Presentation Graphics on the

APPLE® MACINTOSH™

Presentation Graphics on the

APPLE® MACINTOSH™

How to use Microsoft® Chart to create
dazzling graphics for professional
and corporate applications

Steve Lambert

MICROSOFT®
PRESS

PUBLISHED BY
Microsoft Press
A Division of Microsoft Corporation
10700 Northup Way, Bellevue, Washington 98004

Library of Congress Cataloging in Publication Data
Lambert, Steve, 1945-
Presentation graphics on the Apple Macintosh.
Includes index.
1. Computer graphics. 2. Macintosh (Computer)—Programming.
I. Title.
T385.L34   1984   001.64′43   84-8987
ISBN 0-91485-11-X

Printed and bound in the United States of America

1 2 3 4 5 6 7 8 9 HLHL 8 9 0 9 8 7 6 5 4

Distributed to the book trade in the United States and Canada
by Simon and Schuster, Inc.

Contents

Preface

"I would like you to write a book for us. I can't tell you what it will be about—that's top secret information; but after you sign a contract and a nondisclosure statement, I'll have somebody fill you in."

The statement seemed to come from a world of cloaks, daggers, and cassette tapes that self-destruct after thirty seconds; certainly not from the crowd I usually travel with.

I had wandered into the Microsoft corporate complex in Bellevue, Washington, lured by rumors of exciting things happening in their software development department. The short trip was prompted by more than just idle curiosity. I was hoping a little persistent probing would pay off with the opportunity to write a preview review of their soon-to-be-released product. Whatever it was, the first person to produce an article about a new product from Microsoft would have no problem peddling it to the periodicals.

I eventually found myself sitting across a desk from Nahum Stiskin, the person selected by Microsoft to establish them in the publishing business, a task he seemed to be tackling with enthusiasm. After half an hour of friendly but evasive conversation, he leaned back in his chair, looked me in the eye, and delivered the above statement.

I chose to accept the mission. Although my tape recorder did not blow up, the level of secrecy remained on a par with that of *Mission Impossible*. It seemed to take an age to accomplish all the paperwork required for admission to the inner sanctum—one of the longest waiting periods I can recall.

My level of anxiety did not subside when the doors were finally unlocked and I was introduced to my subject. A quick demonstration convinced me that I was going to be writing about a powerful, easy-to-use, inexpensive computer with tremendous potential in the area of business graphics. It was amazing; it was wonderful; it was fascinating. But inwardly I groaned. My subject was to be graphics, a science I knew nothing about. I could appreciate the innovative aspects of the Macintosh computer, and the power of Microsoft's Chart program was impressive; but drawing pictures was an area for a . . . well . . . a graphic designer.

Nahum brushed my objections aside. In his opinion the system was so easy to use that a totally inexperienced operator could turn out beautiful graphs in a matter of minutes. I would be the perfect person to write the book. "Just record your own learning experiences, answer your own questions," he said.

It turned out we were both right: The Macintosh is easy to use and anybody can turn out beautiful graphs. However, the creation of effective business graphics is a blend of art and science that requires a knowledge of more than just which button to push. As I set out in search of this knowledge, I found people who were willing to share the wisdom of their experience with me, and it is this wisdom that I have attempted to pass along to you in this book.

Introduction

The business world floats on and is nurtured by a sea of information. Those who accurately interpret this information thrive and grow stronger; those who don't, drown.

Information, without understanding, is not merely meaningless, it is counterproductive. You can use a chart to distill a large quantity of information and grasp the essence of a complex relationship. You can then pass this essence on to others, in such a manner that they, too, can understand it. You can also, by graphically editorializing the information, influence the beliefs and decisions of others.

In the past, producing meaningful charts was not only time-consuming and tedious, it also required an understanding of mathematics and graphic design. The combination of the Microsoft Chart program and the Apple Macintosh computer now relieves you of all such concerns; anybody can create sophisticated charts and graphs.

A Bit of History

Representing numbers with pictures, though hardly a new concept, is not as old as one might think. The logic behind this method of communication can be traced to René Descartes, the seventeenth-century mathematician and philosopher who lent his name to the Cartesian coordinate system we currently use to plot charts. The idea wasn't exactly a box-office hit, as the civilized world was still dogmatically caught up in Aristotelian reasoning and proponents of "new" thoughts were often called upon to support them with their lives.

It was over a hundred years later, in the late 1700s, that several books were published referring to the use of charts in the study of "history, genealogy, chronology, and matters of finance." Things picked up after that and in 1915 a Joint Committee on Standards for Graphic Presentation was formed in the United States, with hopes of discovering standards that would lead to the more universal acceptance of graphic methods.

The books written on this subject since 1915 have been produced by and for statisticians, mathematicians, and graphic artists. This is a fine group of people and they have done some dandy things with lines and numbers; but with the computer's invasion of the business world and the development of software that puts the production of professional-looking graphs within easy reach, the average business person needs a book that presents graphics standards and techniques in a manner that is relevant and easy to understand, and that takes advantage of the computer and its available software.

What Can You Learn from This Book?

This book illustrates the standards upon which classical charting is based, and shows you how to use the powerful formatting abilities of Microsoft Chart to present your information dramatically and convincingly to others.

Using the proper tool makes any job easier; but it does not ensure that the job will be done properly or that the finished product will represent the craftsman's original intentions. The combination of the Microsoft Chart program and the Macintosh computer is an amazing tool for creating graphs and charts from statistical information; but the fact that this tool is available doesn't mean we are about to be flooded with skillfully created graphic art that will effectively prove its point. After all, the pen existed for some time before Leonardo da Vinci sketched the Mona Lisa. In the world of business graphics, creative ability and care can still make the difference between crystal clarity and confusion.

I can't teach creativity, but I can show you examples of it and explain how to emulate them. I can also explain the standards of graphic presentation that have evolved over the years, and demonstrate methods of meeting these standards with the assistance of a computer.

For the most part, I assume in my discussions that you have a Macintosh computer and the Chart program in front of you as you read. Even if you don't, the screen displays and detailed descriptions will give you a good grasp of how to create business graphs. As you work your way through the following chapters, bear in mind that all illustrations were created on the Macintosh. Most were done entirely with the Microsoft Chart program, though a few had a little help from MacPaint.

Chapter 1 introduces the Macintosh computer and explains how to operate it. If you are already using a Macintosh, you can probably skip this chapter.

Chapter 2 takes you on a quick tour of Microsoft's Chart program. You will create a simple column chart and then convert it to a pie chart. The basic terms and techniques used throughout the remainder of the book are introduced here.

Chapter 3 explains the basic standards that apply to the creation of graphs in any format. The information contained in this chapter is particularly important when you start modifying and enhancing charts.

Chapter 4 provides a detailed description of menu commands in Microsoft's Chart program.

Chapters 5 through 10 illustrate and explain the standards that apply to column, bar, line, pie, area, and scatter charts, and lead you through the creation of several examples of each format using the Macintosh.

Chapter 11 introduces you to some of the other tools available to you when you use the Macintosh, and explains how to integrate them into an effective team.

If you are reading this book to help decide whether to purchase a Macintosh computer or Microsoft's Chart program, I recommend you take this book into a retail dealership, sit down at their demo machine, and discover how easy it is to create these sample charts.

1

The Macintosh Computer

On my first exposure to both the Macintosh and the Microsoft Chart program, I was handed a disk with the program on it, ushered into the room in which the computer resided, and told to "go to it." With neither documentation nor human help, it took a little more than an hour to become comfortable enough with the combination of computer and software to create and modify several charts.

Since using this combination is practically an intuitive process, it probably won't take you any longer to get going than it took me. This introduction to the Macintosh and the introduction to Microsoft Chart in the next chapter are primarily for people who have had no previous exposure to them. If you already have a Macintosh and have used the excellent tutorial provided with it, then you can skip ahead to Chapter 2 and learn about Microsoft's Chart program.

Up and Running

Before you can use Microsoft Chart, you naturally have to get it up and running on the computer.

When you turn on the Macintosh (using the switch on the back of the main unit), the screen displays this symbol, called an icon. This is a request for you to insert a disk, metal end in, label up, in the disk drive.

If you insert a disk that is unformatted, damaged, or does not contain the proper operating system files, the Macintosh both visually rejects it, by Xing out the initial icon, and physically ejects it from the machine.

If you insert a disk containing the Chart program and Apple's operating system (which is included on the Chart disk you purchase), the icon takes on a contented smile.

After accepting the disk, the computer hums melo-diously for a few seconds as it fetches information from the disk. It then presents a display similar to this, called a desktop.

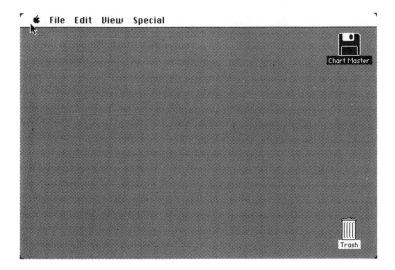

Like an old-fashioned roll-top desk, the Macintosh desktop has drawers at the back to store things in and a work surface in front where you can spread your papers out. We will open these drawers and examine their contents shortly.

At the right side of the initial desktop are two icons. The icon at the top is a disk icon, representing the disk you just inserted in the drive. The name below the icon tells you which disk is inserted; in this case it is your master copy of the Chart program. In a moment we will open the disk icon and display a list of all the programs and files stored on the disk.

The icon in the bottom right corner of the desktop is the Trash icon; here, you dispose of files you no longer need.

There are two methods for passing information and commands to the computer. The most familiar of the two is the keyboard, which varies only slightly from its typewriter equiv-alent and needs no explanation; the other is the mouse, which is a relatively new concept in communication.

The Mouse

The simplicity of the Macintosh's operation is largely due to use of the mouse, both for selecting commands and objects, and for editing words and pictures. To demonstrate the mouse, let's use it to take a tour of the desktop. First, let's move the mouse around a bit and see what happens.

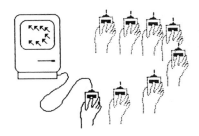

Clear a space on a flat surface next to the computer and slide the mouse around. A pointer on the screen moves in a manner corresponding to your movement of the mouse.

When you slide the mouse, a ball in its base makes contact with the flat surface you are sliding it on and rolls as you move the mouse. It is this rolling ball that controls the movement of the pointer. If you run out of space to slide the mouse, simply lift it and put it down in a different spot—the pointer won't move while the mouse is lifted.

Besides moving the mouse and the pointer around—which may be entertaining but is not particularly useful by itself—you can use them for two important things: selecting commands and objects (such as icons) and moving objects. These uses of the mouse are the same for all Macintosh programs, so I will explain them now and then we will get on with our tour of the desktop.

Making Selections

One use of the mouse is to select a command or an object. Let's select an icon—the Trash icon in the lower right corner of the screen.

To select the Trash icon, position the pointer over it and briefly press and release the mouse button. This action is called clicking. The icon becomes highlighted (background and foreground shades reverse) to indicate you have selected it.

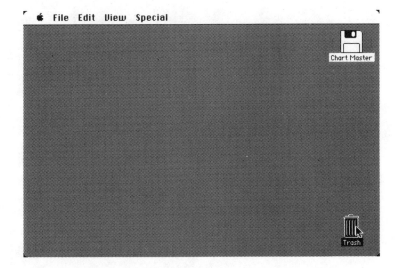

Only one object can be selected at a time. You may have noticed that the disk icon, which is selected automatically when the desktop first appears, changed from black (selected) to white (not selected) when you selected the Trash icon.

If you change your mind after selecting an object, simply click a different icon (to select it instead), or click an empty part of the screen (to select nothing).

Moving Selected Objects

The second use of the mouse is to move things. This action is called dragging, and requires you to move the mouse while you have its button pressed.

Let's drag our Trash icon. Position the pointer over it and hold down the mouse button while you move the mouse. An outline of the icon moves with the pointer. When you release the mouse button, the icon snaps into the location of the outline.

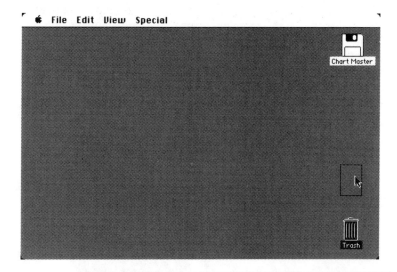

The Command Menus

Most of the work you will do with your Macintosh involves two actions: selecting the object you want to work with, which is usually done by clicking; and telling the Macintosh what you would like done with the object, accomplished by choosing one command from a list, called a menu.

Unlike computers that rigidly require the accurate keyboard entry of complex commands—either mysterious words or strange combinations of letters that must be spelled precisely to avoid error messages and failure—the Macintosh places no great demands on your memory. All the commands you can issue are available for selection with the mouse.

The commands are logically grouped into menus, and each menu has a title. These titles are arranged in a white bar, called a menu bar, across the top of the screen. Going back to our roll-top desk analogy, the titles on the menu bar are like labels on the desk drawers, indicating their contents. You can use the mouse to open the drawers by positioning the pointer over a title and then pushing the button on the mouse. The drawer opens and displays the full menu associated with that title. You can then choose the command you would like to use. Let's have a closer look.

Choosing a Command

Before you choose a command from one of the menus, you must select the object the command will be applied to. For our first command we will open the disk icon, so select the icon by placing the pointer over it and clicking.

Position the pointer so it points to the File menu title and press the mouse button. The drawer opens and reveals its contents—a list of commands and options.

Notice that some of the commands are printed in black and some (such as Close) are in gray.

All commands and options currently available for use are printed in black; the ones that are unavailable are gray. The most common reason a command is unavailable is that you have not selected an object for it to act on.

Holding the mouse button down, move the pointer down the list of commands. Any command printed in black is highlighted as you point to it. You choose a command by releasing the mouse button while the command is highlighted.

Opening an Icon

In order to use one of the application programs stored on the disk, you must first open the disk icon, which is the one you just selected in the upper right corner of the desktop.

Choose Open from the File menu by releasing the mouse button while the pointer is over Open. When you release the button, an outline zooms out of the selected disk icon and rapidly increases in size. After it stops expanding, the outline, called a window, is filled in with a display of icons that represent the programs and documents stored on this particular disk.

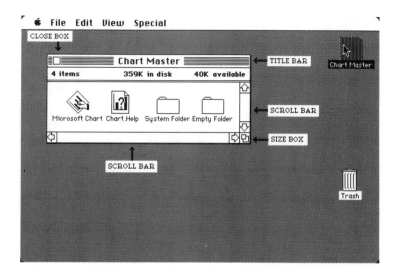

Important parts of the window illustrated here are identified with labels and arrows; how you can use these parts will be explained shortly.

Windows

Windows are used in most Macintosh programs to allow you to look at the contents of documents, charts, drawings, and disks. You will often have more than one window open at a time. Just as you can spread papers out on a real desk, so you can spread windows around the Macintosh desktop, piling them up or putting them away—out of sight—to be taken out again when needed. To keep your desktop neat and orderly, you can change the size and shape of its windows and move them around—all with the mouse.

Changing Size and Shape

To change the size and shape of a window, drag the size box in its lower right corner (place the pointer in the size box, press the mouse button, and move the mouse).

An outline of the window's frame is created and, as you move the mouse, the dimensions of the outline change to keep the moving size box diagonally opposite the upper left corner of the window, which is presently anchored in one spot. When you release the mouse button, the window frame is redrawn on the outline.

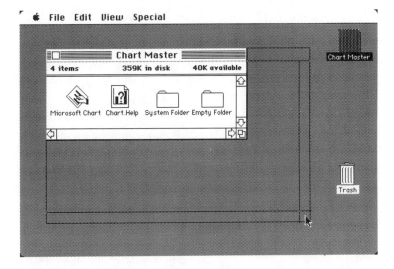

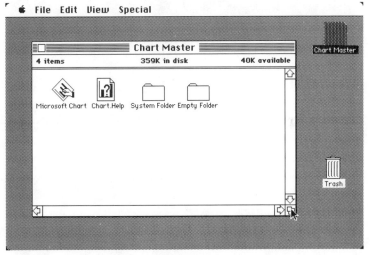

Go ahead and drag the size box around the screen, releasing it at various locations. As you can see, the items in the window don't vary in size; only your view of them—whether you can see them or not—changes. End up with the window filling most of the screen.

Each item stored on the disk is represented by an icon indicating what kind of program or document it is. As you become more familiar with the Macintosh you will learn how to change both these icons and the names below them.

Moving Icons

You can move the icons around the desktop, transfer them between desktops (each disk has a similar desktop), open and use them, or stuff them into the trash can to get rid of them. Manipulating an icon manipulates the program it represents.

Drag the Empty Folder icon to the lower right corner of the window by placing the pointer over it, pressing the mouse button (this selects the icon), and moving the mouse (holding the mouse button down until you are ready to release the icon). Leave the icon in the corner; we'll use it to demonstrate something else in a moment.

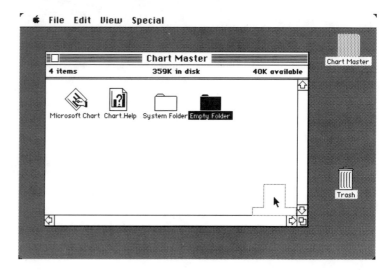

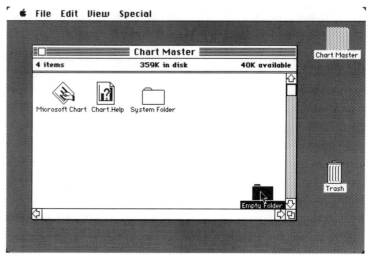

When you want to be able to see the contents of several windows on the desktop at the same time, you have to make each window rather small. You can look at all the icons in a small window by using the scroll bars along the bottom and right side of the window. Make the Chart disk window very small now, by dragging the size box toward the upper left corner of the window; we will then try scrolling through it.

Viewing the Desktop

Let's go looking for the Empty Folder icon we stored in the lower right corner.

Drag the white box in the bottom scroll bar to the right a bit. When you release the mouse button your view through the window shifts; how far it shifts is determined by how far you drag the box.

You can also scroll by clicking the arrow at either end of a scroll bar, placing the pointer over an arrow and holding the mouse button down (to scroll the view continuously in the direction of the arrow), or clicking in the gray bar itself (to scroll a screenful at a time).

Experiment with scrolling; when you scroll all the way down and to the right, you can see the Empty Folder icon.

Moving a Window

You move a window by dragging the title bar that appears at the top of the window. Let's move the Chart disk window to the middle of the desktop.

Position the pointer anyplace in the title bar (other than in the little box at the left edge—this is the close box, used to close the window, a process I will explain in a moment). Press the mouse button and move the mouse; an outline of the window moves with it.

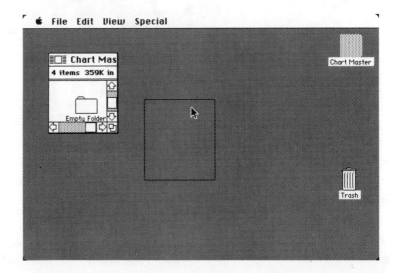

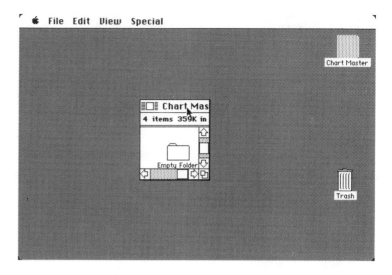

When you release the mouse button, the window is redrawn in its new location. Notice that the visible icons moved with the window, unlike when you scrolled, which exposed different icons.

Multiple Windows

There is a shortcut for opening icons. Let's open the Trash icon, at the right side of the desktop.

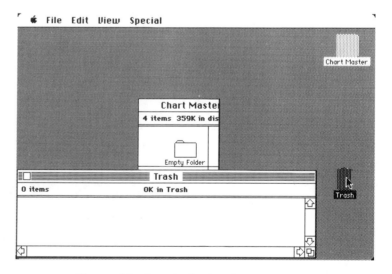

You could select the icon and then choose Open from the File menu as you did with the disk icon, but a faster method is simply to double-click the icon (click it twice, very rapidly). Try it; if the icon doesn't immediately open, try it again, faster.

You end up with two open windows on the desktop: the Chart disk window and the Trash window.

The active window

Did you notice the change in the Chart disk window when you opened the Trash window? The black bands that were in the disk window's title bar disappeared.

Although you can have many windows open at the same time, only one window at a time can be selected to be worked on. The selected window is called the active window, a status indicated by black bands in its title bar. You can designate which window is active by clicking anyplace in it. When you click, the window is selected active and, if it was partially covered by another window, it is brought to the surface. The Trash window you just opened has black bands in its title bar, indicating that it is now the active window.

Position the two windows on the desktop so they overlap, then alternately click in one and then the other and watch the selected window surface. When you tire of watching windows move fore and aft (or get seasick—whichever comes first), we'll close them.

Closing a Window

Just as there are several ways to open windows, there are several ways to close them. One way is to click the close box.

Let's close the Trash window first. If it isn't already selected, click anyplace in it to select it, and then click the close box (the box at the left end of the title bar) and watch the Trash window recede back into its original icon on the desktop.

Another way to close a window is to choose Close from the File menu. Close the Chart disk window now, using this second method.

We will now wrap this session up and quit, just so you'll know how, should the need arise.

Quitting

With all the windows closed, the desktop looks pretty much as it did when you started. If you are going to quit, you should retrieve the disk you inserted to start this session and store it in a safe place. The Macintosh ejects the disk if you tell it to. As with all commands, you must first select the object the command will apply to (the disk), then choose the command

(Eject). The disk icon should already be selected (because you just closed it); if it isn't, click it. Now choose Eject from the File menu. The machine hums to itself for a few seconds as it does some necessary housekeeping chores—making sure all the information on the disk is properly stored away—then it releases the disk and pushes it out at you. You can now turn the power off, or reinsert the disk and join me in the next chapter for a tour of the Chart program.

This was a basic tour of the Macintosh. There are a lot of features we didn't cover, but you now know all you need to know to start using it.

The
Chart
Program

Use your newly developed expertise to turn on the Macintosh, insert the Microsoft Chart disk, and open the disk icon. One of the icons in the window that blossoms onto the desktop is the Chart icon; it shows a hand drawing a chart, with the name Microsoft Chart below it.

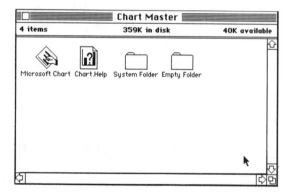

To start the Chart program, you can either double-click the Chart icon, or select it, then choose Open from the File menu. The pointer takes the shape of a wristwatch to remind you that you must wait a moment while the Chart program is brought into the machine.

The Desktop

Chart's desktop is very similar to the Macintosh's—as are the desktops of all other applications. One of the conveniences of the Macintosh is that once you understand the use of one application, you understand the basics of all applications.

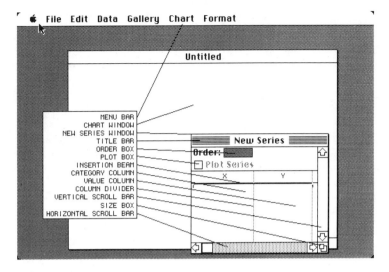

When the disk drive stops whirring and Chart is ready to use, the desktop looks like this. As you can see, the Chart desktop has more titles on the menu bar than the Macintosh desktop, and there are already two windows open.

Each of the menu choices will be discussed in detail in Chapter 4 and explained again in Chapters 5 through 10, as you use them to create charts. In this introductory chapter, I will explain only the commands you actually use to create and edit a simple chart, so that you will have a general idea of how the Chart program works.

Ending a Chart Session

You may not have time to work your way through this chapter in one sitting, so before you get too deeply into Chart, let me tell you how to find your way back out—it's really much easier than leaving a trail of breadcrumbs. The File menu contains commands to fetch previously created charts and to store charts on the disk. It also provides a doorway back to the Macintosh desktop: the Quit command.

Saving Your Work

If you want to end a Chart session in the middle of an example you are creating, you can preserve the work you have done thus far by choosing Save As from the File menu (point to File, press the mouse button, drag the highlight down to Save As, and release the button).

A dialog box

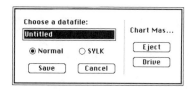

This sequence of commands causes something new to appear on the desktop. Although it has a frame like a window, it isn't a window; it's a dialog box. This is Chart's method of either giving you information or getting information from you.

Chart's dialog boxes have one thing in common—a method of making them go away. You can return to the desktop with no changes by clicking the Cancel button in the dialog box, or continue with the command by clicking an affirmative button, in this case the Save button. Either way, when you click one of these buttons, the dialog box goes away.

Apart from these two buttons, the contents of different dialog boxes vary according to the box's purpose. The purpose of this particular dialog box is to discover the name you want to assign to your chart. The name under which you initially store your chart is automatically provided if you later save an updated version of your chart. This name also appears in the title bar of the window where the chart is plotted.

There are practically no restrictions on what you can name your chart, though you should try to be reasonably succinct to avoid clutter on the Macintosh desktop, where the names of all charts stored on the disk are displayed. A name that brings to mind the subject matter of the chart is also helpful.

The Chart program can store information in one of two modes: Normal or SYLK (which stands for Symbolic Link Format). Notice that the dialog box on your screen has a click mark next to Normal, indicating the proposed mode of storage. Leave the click mark there. The SYLK mode is primarily used to pass information between the Macintosh and other computers that aren't directly compatible with it. We won't use the SYLK mode at all in our examples; for more information about using this mode, refer to Chart's documentation.

If you would like to store the chart on a disk other than the one now in the Macintosh, click the Eject button in the dialog box; the current disk is ejected and you can insert your new one. The program asks you to replace the original disk when it needs it to continue.

If you have a second drive attached to your Macintosh, there is an additional button, labeled Drive, located just below the Eject button. By clicking Drive, you can instruct the program to store your chart on the disk in the external drive.

Quitting

After you have saved your chart, you can choose Quit from the File menu, confident that when the chart is brought back into the program for further modification or printing, all your information will be there.

Two different things can happen when you choose Quit. If you have not changed anything since the last time you saved the information, Chart simply quits, and returns you to the Macintosh desktop.

If you have changed the chart, a dialog box appears, asking if you would like to save your changes. If you click Yes or No, the program returns you to the Macintosh desktop after taking the appropriate action (clicking Cancel returns you to the Chart desktop). Once returned to the main desktop, you can end the session in the manner described at the end of Chapter 1 (close the window, select the disk icon, and then choose Eject from the File menu).

So much for quitting; now let's get on with charting. Just remember where this section is if you need it.

The New Series Window

The two windows that are open when you start the Chart program are the New Series window and the chart window (labeled Untitled), both of which are permanently open. Let's take a tour of the New Series window first.

The New Series window is your starting point for every chart created. The technical aspects of charting will be explained in Chapter 3, but briefly, a chart is created by plotting a number of points and then connecting them with a line, pushing bars out to them, or making them meaningful to the observer in some other manner. Each point to be plotted is called a data point, and the set of data points is called a series. For example, a sales representative might plot her annual sales figures (the series) broken down by dollar volume per month (the individual data points).

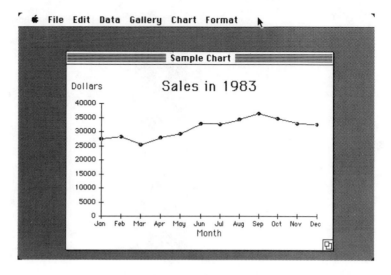

Each data point has two components, one measured along the chart's horizontal axis and the other measured along its vertical axis. In this example the months are measured on the horizontal axis and the dollars on the vertical axis.

You enter into a series window the data points you would like Chart to plot. The horizontal value of the data point (the month) goes in one column, and the vertical value (the dollars) goes opposite it in the other column.

You can plot more than one series at a time on the same chart; the New Series window is used each time you want to add a series. There is no series on your desktop at the moment, so let's create one.

Entering Numbers

If the New Series window is not active (black bands in the title bar), select it by clicking anyplace in it. Now type a bunch of numbers; just so we are all looking at the same display, type these numbers, pressing Enter after each: 12, 23, 34, 45, 56, 67, and 78. When you type the first number you start a lot of different things happening inside the computer, and it may take a few seconds for it to catch up with you—but type as fast as you like; it will eventually catch up.

The Series Window

When you enter the first number, Chart decides this is no longer a new series. It is now an established series that you will be working with, so it is assigned its own series window.

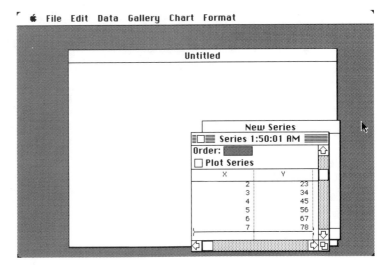

Since every series must have a name, and you have not yet provided one, Chart reads the Macintosh's built-in clock and assigns the current time as the name. So the series window you have just produced probably has a different name from mine—unless we both started at exactly the same time.

Scrolling

Each number you enter in the series window is listed in the right column, opposite a list of numbers Chart enters in the left column. Notice that the numbers scroll under the column headings, X and Y, after the sixth entry.

Remember the scroll bars you used on the Macintosh desktop? The Chart program series windows have identical scroll bars. If you drag the white box in the right scroll bar toward the top of the window, your first few entries are brought back into view. You can also click in the arrow at the top of this scroll bar to scroll up one line at a time.

If you would like a larger series window in order to display more lines at a time, drag the size box in the bottom right corner downward.

Plotting the Numbers

After you have practiced scrolling the numbers up and down in the series window, click the Plot Series button at the top of the left column to plot the data points.

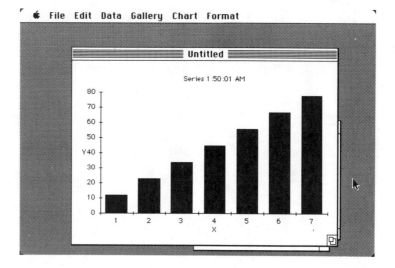

This column chart is drawn in the chart window (the window labeled Untitled that has been lurking in the background all this time). The series name (the time) has been assigned as the chart's name, and a column has been drawn for each of your entries. Part of the chart is covered by the series windows; click anyplace in the chart window to bring the whole chart to the surface. Bringing the chart window to the surface automatically selects it (notice the black bands in its title bar).

The chart you have just plotted is very simple, but the method used to create it is basically the same one you use to create far more complex charts. Now that you have created a series, let me tell you a little more about them.

Series Types

The Chart program is extremely flexible; there are many factors you can control to tailor a chart to your specific needs. Of these factors, some are optional and some must be defined. When a factor must be defined in order to create a chart, the program sets the factor to a predetermined condition and allows you to change it when and if you care to. The series name is such a factor. The series type is another example.

Every series you create is one of four types: sequence, date, text, or number. The series type is automatically set to sequence. In a sequence series, Chart supplies half of each data point by numbering the left column of the series window sequentially from 1 to however many entries you type in the right column. (In a moment, I will show you how simple it is to change the beginning point and the interval of this sequence.)

In a date series, you specify a beginning date and the interval between dates, and Chart enters a sequence of dates in the left column. In a text series or a number series, you have to type in both halves of each data point.

Now that you know you have a sequence series, let's work with it a little. Click the series window to select it and bring it back to the surface. You may have to move the chart window (drag its title bar) or make it smaller (drag the size box) to find the series window.

Choosing the Series Type

Remember how to choose items from the menu? You are going to choose Sequence from the Data menu. Position the pointer over Data in the menu bar, press the mouse button, drag the pointer down to Sequence . . . hold it right there a moment.

Notice the check mark in front of Sequence, indicating that of the four series types listed on the menu, this is the type that matches the currently selected series window.

Now release the mouse button (with Sequence still highlighted) and you are presented with another dialog box.

The Series Properties Sheet

This dialog box contains a Sequence Series properties sheet. One of these sheets is associated with each series, telling what type the series is and storing its name and the names assigned to each of its columns.

As you can see, the series name is the time that was assigned when you created the series, and the category and value names (which appeared above the two columns in the series window) are preset to X and Y.

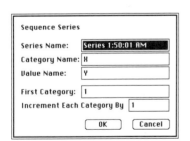

If the series is of sequence or date type, the properties sheet also stores the beginning point of the series and the interval between points. Here the beginning point is shown as 1 and the interval is also 1. Let's change all this.

The Series Name box is highlighted on the properties sheet, meaning that it is selected for editing—its contents will be replaced by anything you type. Type a new name; let's call this Sample Series. If you want to correct a typo, backspace and type the new entry; there are more refined ways to edit, but this will get you by for now. After typing the name, press Tab to move the highlight to the Category Name box.

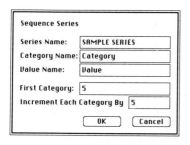

Continue to type and tab, making the same entries on your properties sheet as those you see on mine, until you have changed everything on the sheet. When you have made all the changes, click the OK button to return to the series window and see their effect. (You can click Cancel at any time to return with no changes made.)

When you click OK, the dialog box disappears and the chart and series windows are redrawn, reflecting your changes. Notice that your series name, Sample Series, is on the top line of the series window, and the column names, Category and Value, are above the two columns. Changing the beginning point and the interval to 5 results in an adjustment of the entries previously provided by Chart in the left column of the series window; the sequence now counts by fives, from 5 to 35.

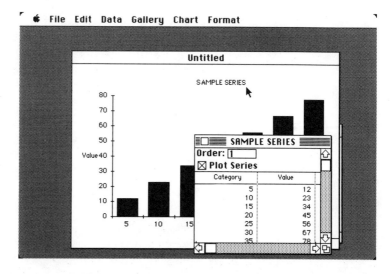

There are two items in the series window that we haven't discussed: the box labeled Order, and the close box in the upper left corner. Let's quickly create another series to demonstrate these features.

Bring the New Series window to the top by clicking anyplace in it, and type the following numbers, pressing Enter after each: 21, 32, 43, 54, 65, 76, and 87. Another sequence series, with its own series window, is created, with the current time as its name. This series will only exist for a few minutes, so don't bother changing its name. Plot your new series by clicking the Plot Series box above the category column (an X appears in the box), and watch as the original chart is redrawn.

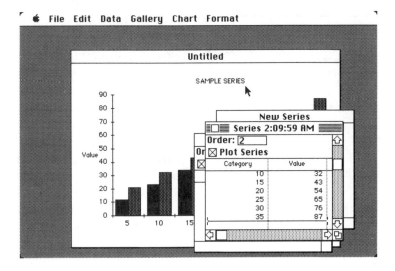

Your desktop should now look more or less like this: two series windows with data points in them, and their plotted equivalent in the chart window.

The Order Box

Notice the number 1 in the order box for your original series, and the number 2 in the box for the second series. These numbers indicate the order in which you clicked the Plot Series boxes, which is also the order in which the columns have been plotted on the chart. (Notice that in each group of two columns, the column belonging to the original series is to the left of the column belonging to the second series.) If you add more series, they will be numbered sequentially, in the order you click the Plot Series boxes in the series windows.

You can change the order in which series are plotted, and therefore the order of the columns in each group, by changing the number in the order box.

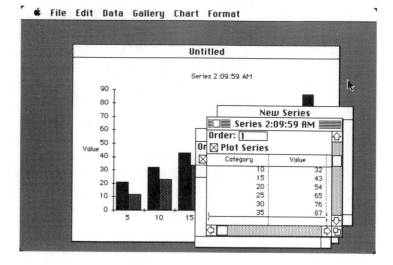

To make this change, first select the order box (place the pointer over it and click). You can then drag through the existing number to highlight it (position the pointer in front of the number, press the mouse button, and slide the pointer through the number), and type a new number to replace it. Edit the order box in the second series window, replacing the 2 with a 1 (press Enter to complete the edit). The desktop is immediately redrawn with a 2 in the order box of the original series window, a 1 in that of the newer window, and the order of the columns on the chart reversed. The title of the chart also changes; until you edit the chart title or an axis label, they are always taken from the first series plotted.

You can edit the order of any number of series. Editing has the same effect as moving one playing card in a stack of cards: all cards between the card's old and new locations shift one position toward the old location to fill the vacated spot.

The Close Box

The close box (the box at the left edge of the title bar) is used to store the series window out of sight. Closing a window doesn't change the information that is stored in it or alter whether it is plotted or not, only whether or not the window is visible on the desktop.

Go ahead and close your newer series window now by clicking its close box. Seems like there should be a puff of smoke when something disappears like that, but I guess that would make everyone nervous.

Opening a Closed Window

When you want to retrieve a closed window, you do so by choosing List from the Data menu (point to Data, press the mouse button, drag down to List, release the button).

When you choose List, this dialog box appears, listing each series you have created (admittedly a short list right now). There are two boxes in front of each series name: one for Show and one for Plot. Clicking these boxes toggles an X on and off in each, and controls whether the window for that series is opened or closed (Show) and whether the series is included on the chart or not (Plot).

Notice that the second series you created (the one with the time for a name) has an X in its Plot box, indicating that it is included on the chart. We really have no further need for it, so click the X to toggle it off and remove this series from the chart. Click OK to confirm your change and get rid of the dialog box. When the desktop is redrawn, only one series is evident—its window is displayed and its data points plotted. The other series is still available but is simply stored out of sight; you could bring it back by again choosing the List command.

There are other things you can do with the series window, but I'll save those for another example. For now let's continue our tour with a closer look at the chart window.

The Chart Window

The chart window is where the action is. After you have entered the data points in the series window and you have clicked the Plot Series button, the data points are automatically plotted in the chart window. Unless you choose otherwise, you get Chart's preset choice of a column chart.

The easiest way to control the type of chart plotted is by choosing a type from the Gallery menu. When you make a choice, a number of parameters that apply to the type of chart you have selected are automatically set. If you don't like the looks of the chart you have chosen, you can choose another.

A more involved method of controlling the chart parameters, which we will discuss later, is to select each parameter on a properties sheet.

Once you have a chart, parts of it can be selected and modified, and the entire chart can be varied in size and moved around the desktop. Let's make a few of these modifications to the simple column chart you have just created. First, let's look at the Gallery menu and see what our options are.

The Gallery

Open the Gallery menu by pointing at it and pressing the mouse button.

This list of chart types appears for you to choose from. The check in front of Column indicates that it is currently chosen. Drag the pointer down to Area and release the mouse button to see the standard area chart formats available.

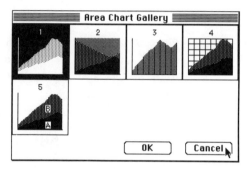

If you would like your data to be displayed in a manner similar to one of the Area Chart Gallery icons, click the icon and then click OK. The Chart program duplicates the chosen format as closely as possible with your data; you can then modify the chart to make it precisely what you want. Let's not create an area chart right now; click Cancel to get rid of this gallery.

Choosing a Format

You can browse through the other galleries if you like, clicking Cancel in each to return to the desktop before choosing the next gallery.

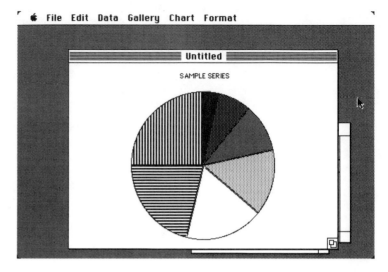

When you get to the Pie Chart Gallery, pick pie number 1 by clicking it; then click OK and watch as your column chart is redrawn. (Click anyplace in the chart window to bring it to the surface and display the entire pie.)

Modifying a Chart

Although this is only a simple pie chart, the program has already made a lot of decisions about it for you—things such as the starting angle of the first segment, the distribution of patterns among the segments, and the size of the circle. You can control these factors and many others, either before or after the chart is drawn. Let's make a few changes to this chart.

Moving objects

If there is a particular segment that you would like to emphasize, one way to draw extra attention to it is by moving it out from the center of the pie.

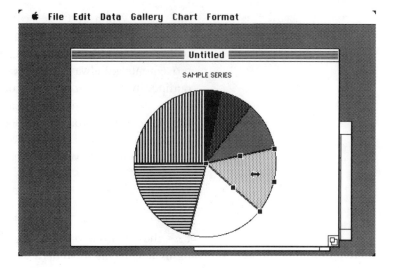

To select the segment you want to emphasize (let's select the fourth from the top, counting clockwise), simply click it. Selecting the segment causes it to be surrounded by little black squares, called handles. The pointer takes on a new shape while it is inside the segment, indicating the directions you can move the segment.

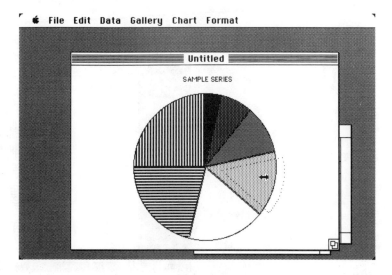

To move the segment, push the mouse button while the pointer is inside the marked segment and move the mouse in one of the two directions indicated by the new pointer. An outline of the segment moves in the same direction.

When you release the button, the segment is redrawn within the outline. Experiment with this a little, and you will find that, at least when dragging pie segments, your mouse movements are always translated into radial movements of the outline, in the direction of one of the pointer's arrows.

You can move, one at a time, as many segments of the pie as you care to. You will soon discover that these methods of movement can be applied to other objects, such as arrows, text, legends, and even entire charts.

Adding text

Let's attribute the data on this chart to a source and tack that information on at the bottom of the chart. You can easily add labels to a chart, and then move them around, edit them, and change their size and shape.

To insert text on the chart, you first show the program where you would like the text to be located (no need to be exact—you can move it later). There are several ways to indicate a text insertion point.

The easiest method is simply to click a blank spot on the chart. A small white cross appears.

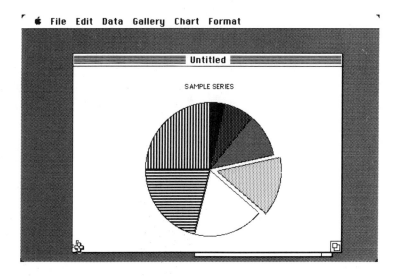

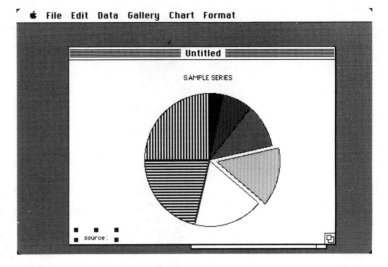

As you type, the cross expands into a frame of black squares surrounding an area that will hold eight characters. If you type more than eight characters, the frame expands more. You can change the size and shape of the insertion space (and thereby change the appearance of the text) by dragging the handles surrounding it.

The second method of inserting text gives you more control over the shape of the space into which the text is inserted. Imagine that you are defining the shape of a box to contain the text. Position the pointer at one corner of the imagined box, then press the mouse button and drag the pointer (which has changed to a double-headed arrow) diagonally to the opposite corner of the imagined box.

As you move the mouse, the outline of a box is dragged out from the place in the window where you originally pushed the mouse button. When you release the button, the outline is replaced by the familiar little black handles indicating an object that is selected.

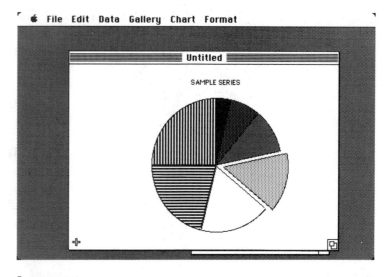

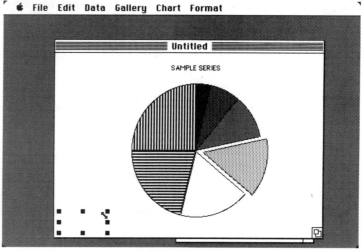

You can now type your text and it will appear within the selected insertion space.

The shape of the insertion space determines how the text you enter is displayed. You can change this space by dragging one of the black handles at its edge (the shape of the pointer while it is over the handle indicates the directions in which the square can be dragged). Each time you change the shape of the insertion space, the text is reformed to fit within that shape, if possible.

After your text is displayed the way you want, you can remove the black handles by selecting something else or by clicking a blank spot in the gray area outside the chart window.

Adding arrows

Another item you can add to the chart, in much the same way as text, is an arrow (or even a whole quiver of arrows).

To add an arrow, you first create another imaginary box (position the pointer, press the mouse button, and drag out the black handled box).

Once the insertion space is defined, simply choose Add Arrow from the Chart menu, and an arrow is instantly drawn. The arrow you add points at the handle where you last released the mouse button, so it normally extends diagonally *from* the corner in which you first pressed the mouse button *to* the opposite corner.

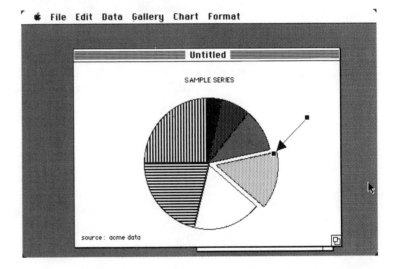

Although you can drag either end of the arrow to point it at various targets on the chart, you may occasionally need a perfectly horizontal or vertical arrow. This need can be satisfied by clicking one of the non-corner handles just before choosing Add Arrow; the added arrow will point from the opposite handle to the handle you clicked.

You can make a variety of format changes to this arrow (as you can to text, the pie segments, the frame and all the other parts of the chart), but I will save the explanation of these changes for another example.

Framing the chart

The last addition you are going to make to this chart is a frame. A frame is particularly important on a pie chart, to keep it from seeming to roll off the page.

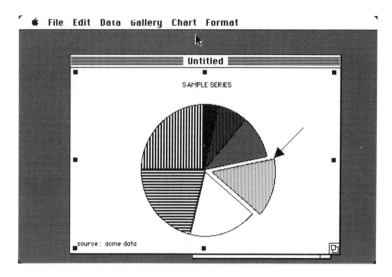

As with your other additions, you first have to show the program where to add the frame. You want the entire chart framed, so choose Select Chart from the Chart menu; the entire chart is surrounded by small black handles.

Although you can't see it, the frame for this chart already exists. Every object on the chart has a frame around it. The frames you don't see have simply been painted with the same pattern as their background, making them invisible.

The pattern of a selected object (in this case the whole chart) can be changed. Choose Patterns from the Format menu and this properties sheet appears.

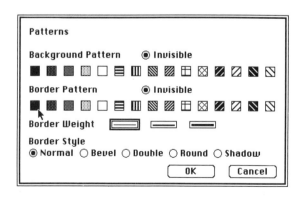

The contents of this sheet vary, depending on the object that was selected when you chose Patterns. In this case it allows you to individually control four aspects of the selected object: the Background Pattern, the Border Pattern, the Border Weight, and the Border Style.

The background and border can each be set to one of fifteen visible patterns, or you can make them invisible (as they now are). The border-weight selection determines the thickness of the visible pattern you choose for the border, and the border-style selection determines the design of the frame.

You will have an opportunity, as you work your way through this book, to try out many patterns and styles. For now, click the solid black border pattern and Shadow border style.

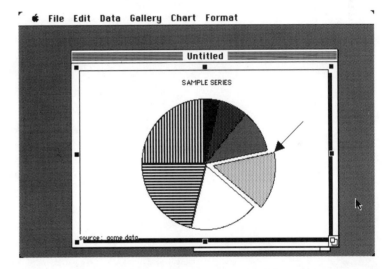

When you confirm your selection by clicking OK on the Patterns properties sheet, the chart is redrawn with your selected frame. While the frame is still selected (as indicated by the black handles), you can, if you like, return to the Patterns properties sheet and try out the other frames.

When you are through framing the chart, click anyplace on the gray desktop; the black selection handles go away.

These are all the changes you are going to make to this chart. You should now be familiar with a few of the features of the Microsoft Chart program, although there are many features you haven't tried. All of these features will be explained in detail in Chapter 4, and applied to specific types of charts in Chapters 5 through 10.

If you would like to continue to experiment with this chart by choosing different options from the menus and seeing what happens, feel free to do so. When you are through experimenting (in a business book like this I can't call it playing), and want to clear your desktop to tackle a new project, you can use the New command from the File menu to help you.

The effect of choosing New is determined by the window currently selected. If a series window is on top, then all data you have entered (in all series windows) is cleared. Format changes you have made to the chart, however, are retained, so any new data you plot appears in the same format. If, on the other hand, the chart window is on top, then all format changes you have made are reset to their predetermined conditions and your data is automatically replotted as a simple column chart. Choosing New twice, once with a series window on top and once with the chart window on top, clears everything—leaving you with a clean desktop.

Clearing the format and data in this manner is a technique you will use often, as you finish one sample chart and prepare to start another.

The Clipboard Window

There is one window we have not yet discussed: the Clipboard window. Like the series windows, the Clipboard window can be opened and closed, so you don't usually have it loitering about the desktop if you aren't using it.

The Clipboard is a part of the computer's memory that is used to temporarily store information that you have just Cut or Copied (two commands from the Edit menu). Information stored on the Clipboard can be Pasted (another Edit command) into another window, either on the Chart desktop or on that of another program. These commands make the Clipboard a useful tool for transferring information within a document or between documents. The use of the Clipboard in conjunction with various menu commands will be explained as the menu commands are explained, so I won't dwell on it here.

Editing Text

Although the Chart program is a picture-processing program, not a word-processing program, you will occasionally have to type in text—either in response to a question in a dialog box, as an entry in a series window, or as an addition to the chart in the chart window. Since perfection is rare (at least among the people I know), there is a possibility you will want to change (edit) something you have typed.

As you enter information, you can do simple text editing by backspacing over letters and typing in the desired change, as you may have done while creating our sample chart. More complex corrections can be easily accomplished with the assistance of the mouse.

To correct existing text you first select the portion you want to work with by dragging through it (position the pointer before the first letter, press the mouse button, move the pointer past the last letter, and release the button). The entire selected text becomes highlighted. Let's give it a try.

I assume you followed my instructions to clear both data and format, and you now have a clean desktop with two empty windows and nothing to edit. Let's create another series, and generate some mistakes to correct.

When you created your first series, you simply accepted the sequence series type, which is the Chart program's preset selection. This time let's be a little more assertive and create a text series. First, make sure that the New Series window is selected (there are black bands in the title bar), then choose Text from the Data menu.

The Text Series properties sheet that appears displays the current time as the series name. Chart has already highlighted the entire entry, assuming you will want to replace it. As you know from the first series you created, what you now type will replace everything that is highlighted.

I would like the name of this series to be This Is My Series. Go ahead and type it in; the new name automatically replaces the previously highlighted title.

On second thought, I think I prefer the name This Series Is Mine. To delete the two middle words, position the pointer in front of I, the first letter to be replaced (the pointer changes shape to an I-beam to indicate that it is over text that can be edited), and press the mouse button; the thin vertical insertion bar that was at the end of the name moves to the location of the pointer. Now, keeping the mouse button depressed, drag the pointer to the space after Y, the last letter to be replaced; all text between the spot where you pressed the mouse button and the current location of the pointer becomes highlighted. Release the button. Now whatever you type will replace only the highlighted center section of the name. If the name was to be This Text Series, for example, you would type the word Text and it would replace Is My between This and Series. However, you don't want anything between Text and Series, so press the Backspace key and the highlighted text disappears.

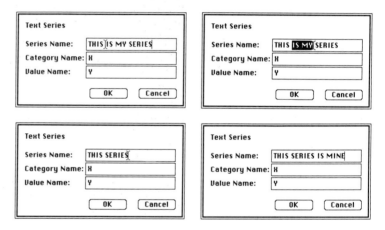

Now move the pointer just past the word Series and click. The thin vertical line that indicates where any text you type will be inserted appears there and you can type a space and the last two words, Is Mine.

So, by clicking between letters you create a point where you can insert new text; by dragging through letters you mark text for replacement.

There is an easy way to select large sections of text for replacement: Select the first character by clicking it and then move the pointer to the last character, hold the Shift key down, and click again. The highlight extends from the first selection to the last. You then either press the Backspace key to delete the highlighted text or type something new to replace it.

These are the basic techniques for text editing in the Chart program. As you continue with this book you will be introduced to additional commands that can be applied to your highlighted text, but the methods of selecting the text for editing will remain the same.

An Introduction To Graphing Techniques

The human mind can comprehend a visual representation far faster, and retain it far longer, than the words and numbers required to adequately explain the same relationship.

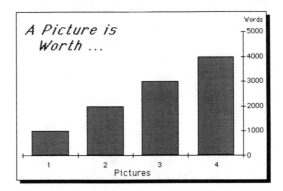

However, the shopworn statement illustrated by this graph is no longer totally accurate. In this age of instant gratification, the average person doesn't really want to read a thousand words; it is probably more realistic to say that a picture is worth ten minutes of discussion.

Creating Effective Graphs

To be effective a graph must capture your intended audience's attention and hold it while clearly communicating your message. The probability of this happening is increased if you plan and prepare your graph in a logical manner consistent with established standards. In this chapter I will describe preparation techniques you can apply to all graphs; subsequent chapters will deal with techniques specific to each type of graph you can create with the Microsoft Chart program.

Step One: Identify the Point

The first step toward creating effective business graphs is deciding precisely what point you would like to prove or what elusive fact you would like to force out into the open. A graph is an editorialized comment, weighted heavily by your opinion or point of view. The same information can be used to create a variety of graphs with implications varying from positive to negative to nonsense. Just as your tone of voice and body language can influence those who hear and see you, so can your choice of scale and shading affect those who see your graphs.

The information you choose to leave out of a report can sometimes be just as influential as that which you include. I remember reading about an article released by the Soviet news agency Tass, reporting on the outcome of an international sporting event. The valiant home team, it stated, had finished second, while the American Imperialists had ended up in the next to last position. The significant missing fact, from our point of view, was that there were only two teams in the competition.

Step Two: Select a Format

Once you determine the purpose of your graph, the next step is to select an appropriate format from your bag of tricks. Selection is based on an evaluation of the type of data available, the presentation medium to be used (such as book, magazine, or overhead projection), and the size and experience level of the intended audience.

For example, a presentation designed for people who have a basic understanding of your subject and are comfortable interpreting graphs can feature complex multi-line graphs that point out subtle variations that might otherwise escape detection. Scatter graphs, logarithmic scales, and exotic mutations of the standard formats, appropriate for this audience, are not as meaningful for a less sophisticated group. A presentation designed for visitors who may only have a casual interest in your subject is better expressed with pie, bar, and column charts.

The graphs prepared for an informal presentation to six or eight people could be effectively displayed on the computer screen in a slide-show format. On the other hand, the same display for 40 or 50 people, or for a presentation in a remote location, might require a show with real slides—actual photographs of the computer's screen that could be projected onto a large screen for easy viewing.

A tremendous advantage of using the computer to create graphs is that you can compare innumerable variations on the same theme, then pick the one you like best and discard the rest. In addition, once a selection is made, you can play around with it on the screen—adding title, subtitle, labels, lines, arrows, and so on—and then either store it on a disk for future use or send it to a reproduction device, such as a printer, plotter, video tape recorder, or slide camera.

Step Three: Check for Accuracy

The last stage in this creative effort is simply sitting down and calmly looking your graphs over—even if you are late for the meeting at which you plan to display them. Check the spelling, punctuation, capitalization, and overall appearance; but most important, check for numeric accuracy! This is probably the only exclamation point I will use in this book, but the statement warrants it. It amazes me that some people spend days gathering numbers and then don't bother to make sure the right numbers actually make their way into a report.

I witnessed an excellent example of the consequences of lack of review several years ago. I had dropped in for an early morning cup of coffee with a friend who was an executive with a major West Coast chain of retail stores. The stock market had been open for several hours on the East Coast and there was alarm and puzzlement evident among the early arriving employees regarding the action of the company's stock. Its steady upward creep had been interrupted that morning by a seemingly inexplicable plunge of several points. The cause was discovered when a reporter called to confirm the figures in a preliminary annual report released the day before. It turned out that during preparation of the report, a copy of the previous year's report had been given to a staff member with instructions to "make it just like this." The accompanying list of updated numbers disappeared and the instruction was followed too literally. The report, which was identical to the previous year's, was approved by three people, each of whom should have spotted the radical reversal in the company's growth trend but didn't. Fortunately, the company's recovery was as rapid as their fall and no lasting harm was done—other than to a few egos.

Available Formats

There are a variety of formats available for presenting quantitative data either to prove your point or to discover just what your point is. In the next several chapters I will discuss the standards that apply to column and bar charts; line, area, and scatter graphs; and pie charts. You can follow along as I use Chart on the Macintosh to create an example of each basic format, and modify these examples into a few not-so-basic formats.

Before we get into the standards and techniques specific to each format, here are a few general guidelines that apply to all formats.

Standards

In 1915 the Joint Committee on Standards for Graphic Presentation was convened with the objective of establishing standards for the creation of graphs. The passage of time has eroded the standards they established, and changes in taste and methods of production have further modified these standards into a softer set of guidelines.

Microsoft's Chart program sticks pretty close to these guidelines when creating a basic graph in any format. Since you will probably want to embellish or refine these basic graphs, I will review, explain, and show you examples of the standards. The computer will not force you to stay within these guidelines, but doing so will make your graphs more credible and comprehendible to the people who read and interpret them.

Axes

There are two types of variables connected with a graph: an independent and a dependent variable, referred to in the Chart program as the category and the value. The program automatically assigns each variable you enter to the appropriate axis and plots the points. Which variable goes on which axis is determined by the type of graph you instruct Chart to create.

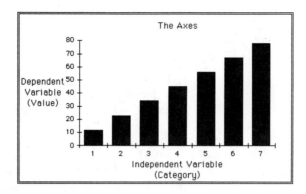

Column, line, and area graphs measure the category (independent variable) along the horizontal or X-axis, also known as the abscissa. The value (dependent variable) is measured along the vertical or Y-axis, also known as the ordinate.

The bar chart reverses this relationship, measuring the category along the vertical axis and the values along the horizontal axis. Pie and scatter graphs have their own methods of expressing this relationship, which I will discuss when describing these formats.

Chart automatically establishes these relationships and plots the points within seconds. Doing the same thing by hand would be tedious and time consuming, as I will demonstrate with a simple example. After you have created a few graphs using Chart, you will begin to appreciate the power that is at your fingertips.

Suppose you want to show how the median income for families in the United States changed between 1955 and 1980 and you have looked the following information up in the *Statistical Abstract of the United States:*

Year	1955	1960	1965	1970	1975	1980
Income	4599	5873	7330	10516	14867	23141

The type of information that each graphic format is best at displaying will be discussed in the chapter specific to each format. For now, simply accept the fact that a change in value over a series of equal time periods can be properly expressed with either a column chart or a line graph. Since there are only six data points to plot, a column chart will adequately illustrate the change; if there were several dozen points, this format would be too crowded and a line graph should be used.

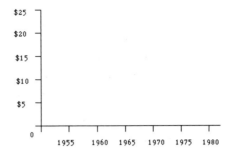

To present your data in column-chart format, you first create a category scale along the horizontal axis by making one mark (called a tick) for each of the years to be plotted. You next mark the increments for the dollar values along the vertical axis, starting with zero at the bottom and measuring off equal increments up to a value that is just higher than the largest dependent variable to be plotted.

Since the range of values for this variable is $4,599 to $23,141, increments of $5,000 extending up the scale to $25,000 would be appropriate.

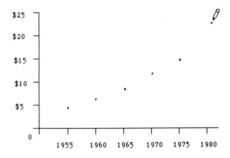

You create the graph by plotting the value of the dependent variable (income) that corresponds to each increment of the independent variable (year); that is, by putting a mark within the plot area at the point of intersection of imaginary lines drawn horizontally from the income value on the vertical axis and vertically from the year on the horizontal axis.

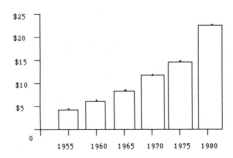

Since this is a column chart, you next draw a column for each year, extending it upward from the horizontal axis to the point you have just plotted. If you were creating a line graph rather than a column chart, you would have simply connected the plotted points with a series of straight lines.

Scaling the axes

When marking your measurements along the value axis, it is best to use units of 1 or 2, or some multiple of 5 or 10—numbers people are comfortable working with mentally.

Take care when selecting the units of measurement and the distances between the units for both axes. As can be seen in these different plottings of the same values, it is possible to completely change the apparent value of a graph by selecting different scales and distances.

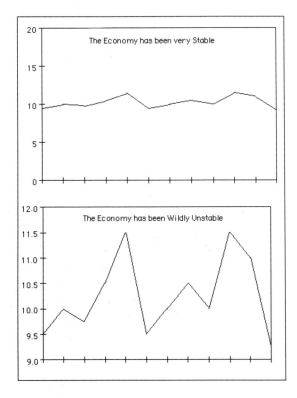

A rule of thumb is that the vertical axis should be about three-quarters the length of the horizontal axis. Since most people have two thumbs, I'll give you another rule of thumb: the horizontal axis should be 1.414 times the vertical. Isn't precision wonderful? Using the second rule, if I have a graph with a vertical axis of 4 inches, the horizontal axis should be 5.656 inches. Drawing a line exactly that length takes a steady hand and a calibrated eye . . . or Chart, which allows you to set measurements and movements as precisely as you care to.

I shouldn't make fun of such rules; I'm sure many people take them seriously—especially the people who wrote them. I'm just trying to point out that few things are totally inflexible. A graph is a mixture of art and science—in Bertrand Russell's words, a geometric metaphor.

The numbers you chart may express pinpoint accuracy, but the rules governing their display are open to your interpretation—although too much latitude in interpretation may lead to accusations of deception rather than perception.

Labels

To be informative, a chart must be labeled with words, numbers, and other symbols; but to be effective, their use should be kept to a minimum and their size and typeface should be consistent.

There is a hierarchy to this labeling; size, weight (how thick the lines are), and shading are proportional to the importance of the label to the chart.

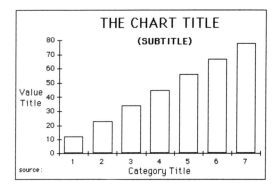

As you can see here, the title, in the largest letters used on the chart, appears at the top, either centered or aligned with the left edge. If a subtitle is required to qualify or support the title, it is placed beneath the title, in smaller or lighter lettering. If the title is not centered, the subtitle can either be aligned with it or offset to the right for balance.

Labels for lines, bars, and segments are next in importance. These are followed by the horizontal and vertical grids and the scale captions.

If possible, the captions, such as "Midwestern States" or "Industrial Pollution," that identify the dependent and independent variables should be printed horizontally. Chart allows you to insert vertical labels, but don't exercise this option any more than you have to. The X-axis caption is centered below the axis; the one for the Y-axis should be centered on the axis or placed just above it.

You can dispense with the category caption (on whichever axis it appears) when plotting values for a series of dates that divide the axis into equal time intervals. The interval labels—Jan, Feb, Mar, or Mon, Tue, Wed—should be adequate to identify the category for the reader.

When identifying each increment on the horizontal axis, be sure to place the label directly below the plotted point, whether that point is on a grid line or between lines.

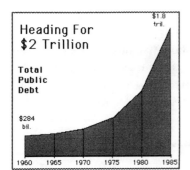

The units of measurement on the value axis should be clearly identified ("thousands of hours" or "millions of people"). If your chart is scaled in "billions or trillions of dollars," make sure it's obvious; many people still have difficulty dealing with more than six digits in front of the decimal point. About the only time you might deal with such large numbers is when discussing distances to other solar systems, or the national debt.

For added credibility, identify your source of information at the bottom of the chart in the smallest lettering used, aligning it with the left edge. Any other necessary notes can be placed on the right to balance the source.

Don't leave off any information just because it is included in the accompanying text; everything required to interpret the graph should appear on it.

Legends

Graphs can be used to compare different groups of numbers by placing several graphs side-by-side, or by plotting more than one group on the same graph.

When a graph has more than one series plotted on it, each series is represented by a different pattern. This pattern can be the shape of the markers on a scatter or line graph, or the shading of the bars, columns, or pie segments on those formats.

Each series can be labeled, with a title and an arrow pointing to a typical segment, or a legend can be used. A legend, often called a key, is composed of a sample of each pattern with the title of the series for which it stands.

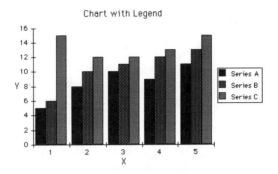

Chart with Legend

You can place this legend, with or without a frame around it, at the side of the graph or above or below the plot area. Consider the balance of the graph when deciding whether to use a legend and where to place it.

Contrast

Your finished chart should stand out from any surrounding text. Whether this is accomplished with patterns, framing, or the judicious use of white space, the more the chart is distinguished from its background, the greater will be the reader's perception of it.

Unity

A good graph should have contrast—both with its field and between its components—but it should also have unity. There should be some logic to the variations used to create contrast. Using the same sequence of patterns throughout a presentation is one method of maintaining unity.

Framing your graph will also give it visual unity and tie it down to the page. Chart provides a basic selection of frames that can be used "as is," or altered for the desired effect.

Balance

There should be a balance, both within the graph and with the rest of the page. Balance is achieved by changing the relative positions of titles, legends, and descriptive text. Simply varying the thickness of lines, the shapes used, or the shading will also affect the balance.

Contrast, unity, and balance are interrelated; the effect of varying one of these on the others should be considered.

But Most Important . . .

Above all else remember: Neatness counts. It shows you care about the material you are presenting.

Besides these general guidelines each format has its own rules. In the following chapters I will apply the general guidelines to each format and also explan any additional rules specific to that format.

Truly creative people become rich and famous by disregarding standards and adding their own imaginative flair to everything they do; on the other hand, some people who think they are truly creative become unemployed with the same flair. If you don't have absolute confidence in your creative genius, I suggest you follow the guidelines.

The
Chart
Commands

This chapter presents a detailed discussion of the commands in Chart's menu bar. The commands will be discussed in the order they appear on the screen (left to right on the menu bar, top to bottom of each menu).

If you are really anxious to get on with creating charts you can skip ahead to the hands-on sections in Chapters 5 through 10, where each command is also explained as it is used.

Menu Conventions

To look at the commands available in a menu, position the pointer over the menu title and press the mouse button. A box listing that menu's commands drops from the menu bar.

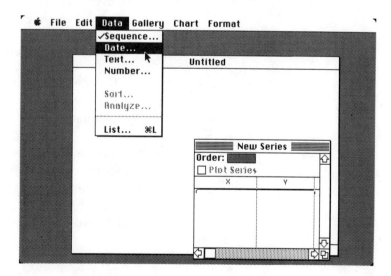

There are several conventions followed in all the menus. As you saw in Chapters 1 and 2, the commands that are currently available are displayed in black; those that are not currently available, usually due to the sequence in which events occur, are displayed in gray.

If you drag the pointer down the list, the available commands become highlighted (displayed in white on a black background). You choose a command by releasing the mouse button while the command you want is highlighted.

Some commands are followed by an ellipsis (three dots). When you choose one of these commands, you are presented with a dialog box requesting additional information.

Other commands are preceded by a check mark. These commands are turned on or off by choosing (clicking) them; the check mark indicates that they are on.

The Apple Menu

```
🍎
About Microsoft Chart...

Scrapbook
Alarm Clock
Note Pad
Calculator
Key Caps
Control Panel
Puzzle
```

This menu, headed by its little apple icon, is a compilation of useful programs, called desk accessories, provided by Apple. The Apple menu is included in most application programs for the Macintosh.

You can interrupt what you are doing in the Chart program to summon one (or more) of these accessories to the desktop; when it has served its purpose, you can dismiss it and continue charting. If you are making frequent use of one accessory, you can even leave it on the desktop while you go on with other tasks. Let's take a closer look at these accessories.

About Microsoft Chart ...

The only entry on this menu that is unique to the Chart program is the first one: About Microsoft Chart. This is your access point for an on-disk help file that can ease you over any rough spots encountered while creating a chart. When you choose this selection from the menu, you are presented with a dialog box listing the topics for which help is available. You can scroll through the list and click the topic you need help with, which produces another dialog box with information that is specific to that topic.

Scrapbook

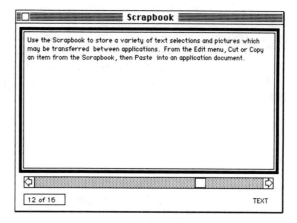

You can store text and pictures in this electronic Scrapbook just as you can store newspaper clippings and snapshots in your bulkier paper equivalent. You can paste information into the Scrapbook that you have previously cut or copied to the Clipboard, or you can cut or copy information from the Scrapbook to the Clipboard and then paste it into another document. For example, you can accumulate charts here during a charting session, and then transfer them as a group to the MacPaint or MacWrite program.

Alarm Clock

This Alarm Clock displays the time and date that are kept by the system clock. The system clock is powered by a battery in a compartment at the back of the Macintosh, so it keeps accurate time even when you are not using the computer. The system time can be set either with this Alarm Clock, or at the Control Panel (the next-to-last selection on this menu).

You can set the Alarm Clock so that it beeps at a selected time; the alarm going off also causes the Apple icon to blink until the alarm is reset. If the Macintosh is not turned on at the time the alarm is set to go off, the beeping and blinking occur the next time you turn the machine on.

The time and date from this clock can be copied onto the Clipboard and pasted from there into the Scrapbook and other applications.

Note Pad

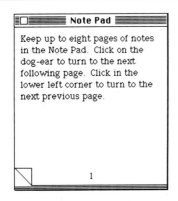

This useful accessory serves the same purpose as the backs of old envelopes and other pieces of scrap paper. You can interrupt any application program to type a note here, and then return to what you were doing. Your notes are saved in a file on the disk, and can be cut and pasted into other documents through the Clipboard.

Calculator

You can use this Calculator just as you would the one you carry in your purse or pocket. The results of your mathematical manipulations can be copied onto the Clipboard and pasted back into other documents.

Key Caps

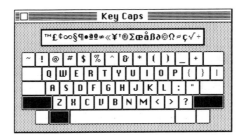

This display is more useful than it at first seems, as it is capable of displaying the alternate type symbols available from the keyboard (some of these special symbols are shown in the panel above the keyboard). If you press the Option key while looking at this display, the familiar key symbols change to the symbols produced when the keys are pressed in combination with the Option key.

Control Panel

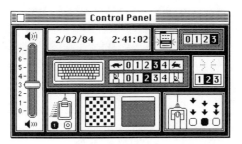

Choosing this panel allows you to control various audio-visual aspects of the computer. The time and date, the volume of the speaker, the pattern of the background, and some keyboard and mouse functions are set here. For a complete explanation of these controls, read the Macintosh manual.

Puzzle

Choosing Puzzle produces this familiar little game. If you are about to be caught playing with this when you should be working, you can make it disappear by clicking the close button in the upper left corner.

The File Menu

Pressing the mouse button while pointing at File displays commands that can be used to move information into and out of the program. Information can be brought in from other charts created with this program, or from documents created by other programs and stored in a compatible format (the technical section of Microsoft's Chart manual gives more information on data storage formats). You already used the New, Save, and Quit commands while creating the chart in Chapter 2; here are more details.

New (Data or Format)

Choosing New from the File menu allows you to selectively clear the data and format changes you have entered during the current charting session. If a series window is selected (if it is on top of the stack of windows on your desktop), the menu choice is New Data, and choosing it clears all series windows. If the chart window is selected, the menu choice is

New Format, and choosing it resets all format changes to Chart's original settings, causing any existing data to be replotted as a simple column chart. You can clear both data and format by choosing New with one window on top, bringing the other window to the top, and choosing New again.

Open ...

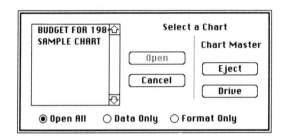

Releasing the mouse button with the pointer on Open produces this dialog box, allowing you to bring a chart you have previously saved back into the program for printing or further modification.

The window, called a mini-finder, at the left side of this dialog box lists the documents stored on the currently selected disk that you can open. You open a document by clicking its name and then clicking the Open button, which turns from gray to black after you have selected a name.

You can also specify, by clicking the appropriate option, whether you would like only the data brought in, or only the format. If you don't specify one or the other, the preselected Open All brings both in. Data brought into the program in this way does not destroy existing data; data points brought in from other documents are placed in series windows and can then be integrated into your existing chart. Formats brought into the program, on the other hand, replace any format parameters you have set in this session. Transferring the format allows you to create a complex format in one document, and then rapidly apply it to different sets of data.

The dialog box's Eject button allows you to eject the current disk and insert another. The files on the new disk then appear in the mini-finder and the name you have assigned to the disk appears above the Eject button. This allows you to store your data files (charts, letters, drawings, and so on) on a disk other than the one containing the application program that created them—a useful feature, as program disks usually have little storage space available.

If you are using the Chart program on a Macintosh that has an external drive, the dialog box has an additional button, labeled Drive, located just below the Eject button. Clicking the Drive button replaces the list of files in the minifinder with those on the disk in the external drive, allowing you to select one and open it.

If you change your mind about opening a new document, you can click the Cancel button at any time and return to the desktop with no changes.

Close

The effect of choosing Close is the same as individually selecting a window and clicking its close button. This command has no ellipses after it, indicating that it goes into effect instantly, with no intermediate dialog box.

A closed window still exists on the desktop; it has simply been stored out of sight, and can be opened with the List command from the Data menu.

Save

The Save command is only available (printed in black rather than gray) when you are working on a document you have already named with the Save As command. Choosing Save replaces a previously stored version of the chart you are working on with the current version. If you would like to keep both versions, you have to use the Save As command so that you can give the new version a different name.

Save As ...

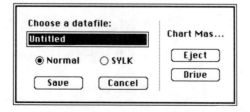

When you choose Save As, you are presented with this dialog box, allowing you to name your chart.

As I've mentioned, Normal and SYLK (Symbolic Link Format) refer to the manner in which the chart information is stored on the disk—normal being, appropriately, the normal method. Symbolic storage is used when you intend to transfer the stored information to a computer other than another Macintosh. The *Microsoft Chart* manual contains additional information about the SYLK format.

If you click the Save button, the chart is saved on the currently inserted disk. You can click Eject and then insert a different disk before clicking Save, or, if you have a two-drive system, you can click Drive and store the chart on the disk inserted in the external drive.

Page Setup ...

Paper:	⦿ US Letter	◯ A4 Letter		OK
	◯ US Legal	◯ International Fanfold		
Orientation:	⦿ Tall	◯ Tall Adjusted	◯ Wide	Cancel

Page Header: [   ]
Page Footer: [   ]

Left Margin: [1]   Right Margin: [1]
Top Margin: [1]   Bottom Margin: [1]

At the top of this dialog box you are given the opportunity to specify both the size of paper you will be printing on and the direction you want the information (text or chart) printed; clicking Wide causes the image to be printed lengthwise on the paper, rotated 90 degrees in a clockwise direction from the image you see on the Macintosh screen.

The center section of the dialog box allows you to provide text that will appear at the top (a header) and bottom (a footer) of each page. You can control the placement of this text and the insertion of the page number, date, and time, by embedding codes in the text.

- &L aligns to the left (left justifies)

- &R aligns to the right (right justifies)

- &C centers

- &P inserts the page number

- &D inserts the date

- &T inserts the time

Each code applies to the text that follows it, and stays in effect until another code is detected. If, for example, you specify the header:

&LThis chart was printed at &T on &D. &Rpage &P

your printer will print the following at the top of the page:

This Chart was printed at 10:45 PM on 2/13/84.   page 1

The bottom section of the Page Setup dialog box allows you to set the margins. By setting the margins, you control not only the chart's placement on the printed page, but also its size, as the chart will be scaled to fit the available space.

Print (Data or Chart) ...

Quality:	○ High	⦿ Standard	○ Draft	OK
Page Range:	⦿ All	○ From:	To:	
Copies:	1			
Paper Feed:	⦿ Continuous	○ Cut Sheet		Cancel

The print command is applied to the information contained in the top window on the desktop, and the wording of the command changes to remind you which window you are about to print. To print your chart, select the chart window before choosing Print; to print a series, select its window first.

This dialog box, presented when you choose Print, allows you to select the print quality—High, Standard, or Draft—desired and to specify the range of pages to be printed, the number of copies, and the type of paper feed.

All three levels of print quality can be applied to text (such as a series window), but only High and Standard apply to charts. You should try all three levels of print quality to see which best suits your needs; but you will probably find that Standard is the one you will use most often. The High print quality selection produces a sharper, blacker image that reproduces well, but it takes quite a bit longer to print.

Since charts are scaled to fit on one page, the Page Range option applies only to text, so should be left set on All when printing a chart. If you are printing a long list of numbers from a series window, or have the margins set so there is only a small area left for text to be printed, the program divides the text into pages and prints the pages you specify in the From: To: section of the Page Range entry.

If you specify Cut Sheet for the Paper Feed option, the printer pauses after every page and asks you to insert the next sheet of paper.

Quit

This is the end of the line. If you have charted all your data and are ready to call it a day, do so by choosing the Quit command. If you have made no changes since the last Save, you leave the Chart program and are immediately returned to the Macintosh desktop.

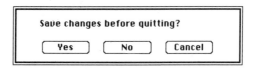

If you have made changes to either the data or the format, this dialog box appears, asking if you would like to save the changes and giving you the opportunity to cancel the Quit command and return to your chart.

The Edit Menu

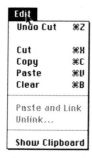

You use the edit commands primarily to move or delete lines in the series windows and occasionally to delete text or arrows from a chart or to copy a chart. These commands not only give you the power of the old-time editor's scissors and paste pot, they add the modern convenience of a copy machine and the unheard of luxury of letting you change your mind and take back a previous command.

Making editorial corrections or changes to text in a series window (without moving it to another line), or on a chart, requires no commands from the Edit menu—you simply select the text and type its replacement.

Undo

Some of our mistakes we have to live with; others are more transitory in nature. The Undo command gives you the chance to change your mind after typing text or issuing a Cut, Copy, or Paste command. Wishy-washy people can even undo an Undo—the possibilities for vacillation are almost unlimited.

The wording of the Undo command always indicates what it is capable of undoing at that moment. For example, after cutting something it changes to Undo Cut, after copying, it changes to Undo Copy.

Cut

Cutting, as its name implies, removes something from its present location. You can cut one or more lines from a series window (up to the entire series, in which case you are asked if you would like the series deleted). You can also cut text and arrows from the chart window. The piece of information that you cut is stored on the Clipboard, until it is replaced by the next piece of information you cut.

To cut an allowable item (text or arrows) from a chart, first select it by pointing and clicking, and then choose Cut from the Edit menu; the chart is redrawn without the item.

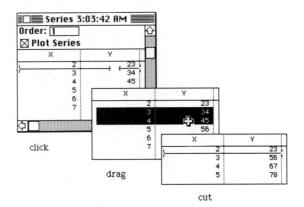

To cut one or more lines from a series window, first place the pointer above the top line to be cut and press the mouse button (a thin line appears at the pointer position); then drag the pointer to the last line to be cut and release the button (the entire section is highlighted). You can then choose Cut from the Edit menu. The highlighted lines disappear from the series window and reappear on the Clipboard.

Copy

The Copy command temporarily stores information on the Clipboard, just as the Cut command does, but the information is not deleted from its original location. To copy something, you first mark it in the same manner as for cutting, and then choose the Copy command. If a series window is selected anything from one line to an entire series can be copied to the Clipboard and then pasted back into another series window, the Scrapbook, or another document.

If the chart window is selected when you open the Edit menu, the Copy command appears on the menu as Copy Chart. Choosing the command now copies the chart window to the Clipboard; from there it can be pasted into the Scrapbook or another document.

Paste

The Paste command is used to re-insert information from the Clipboard. The Cut or Copy and Paste commands can be used to rearrange the lines of data points in a series window, to combine series windows, to duplicate series windows, and to move charts between documents. The Paste command copies but does not remove items from the Clipboard, so the same information can be pasted into several locations.

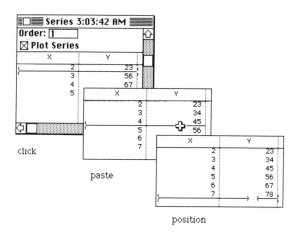

To re-insert one or more lines of text that have been sent to the Clipboard, place the pointer between the lines where you want the text inserted and click; the thin H-beam appears.

Then choose Paste from the Edit menu. After the lines are pasted, you can reposition the H-beam to the bottom of the series (by clicking there) to make additional entries.

Clear

Choosing Clear removes information from the screen without sending it to the Clipboard. This is a useful command if you're not quite ready to paste the Clipboard contents someplace, but don't want to bump them out of the Clipboard with a new cut or copy.

Paste and Link

The Paste and Link command is used to transfer information from another chart or from Multiplan, and to permanently link the information to its source. Each time you load a chart that contains linked information, the program opens the source document (the other chart or the Multiplan file) and updates the linked information. This is useful if you are working with information that is subject to frequent change (such as the value of the stocks in your portfolio), and want to manipulate it in a spreadsheet and plot it in several formats. You only have to type the changes once in the spreadsheet; all the linked versions are automatically updated.

The actual link is performed by bringing up the source program, copying the information to the Clipboard, quitting the source program and bringing up Chart, and choosing Paste and Link. The information is pasted from the Clipboard into the New Series window, or into another series window you have prepared for it.

Unlink ...

The Unlink command breaks the link you previously made between a chart and another source of information.

When you select a linked series and then choose Unlink, a dialog box displays the source of the linked series and asks you to confirm that you want the link broken.

Show Clipboard

The Show Clipboard command is used either to open the Clipboard window or, if it is already open but is lost in the clutter, to bring the Clipboard window to the top of the stack of windows on your desktop.

The Data Menu

The Data menu commands allow you to enter information about a series, such as titles and type, and to manipulate and analyze the data points to be plotted.

Information that affects the plotted appearance of each series is stored on a set of properties sheets that stays with the chart when it is saved on the disk. One kind of properties sheet records information about the series type. As you know from Chapter 2, there are four types of series: Sequence, Date, Text, and Number. Each has specific properties. When you choose one of these series types from the Data menu, its properties sheet appears so you can enter relevant information.

Sequence ...

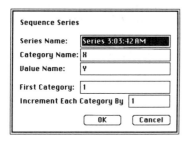

The series type for the New Series window (which is always someplace on your desktop) is preset to Sequence. When entering information into this type of series, you need only enter the value half of each data point; Chart provides the category half—computed from the first category and increment stored on this properties sheet.

When you create a series (either by entering data into the New Series window or by choosing a series type from the Data menu), the current time is automatically assigned as the series title. In Chapter 2, you saw how to change this title to something more appropriate by typing a new title while the old one is highlighted on the properties sheet. When you are satisfied with the title, the highlight can be moved to the next line by pressing the Tab key.

The title you assign appears at the top of the series window and, if this is the first series plotted on this chart, is also the title for the chart itself. You can, of course, select the chart title and change it, if another title is more appropriate.

The category and value names you assign on the properties sheet head the two columns in the series window and will be the axes titles when you plot the data.

The First Category and Increment have default values of 1, meaning that Chart provides category labels of 1, 2, 3, 4, 5 . . . and so on. You can change these numbers to any other values—positive or negative, whole or decimal—though it is best to keep them as simple as possible so the person viewing your chart can understand the logical nature of the sequence and interpolate the values between the listed labels.

Clicking the OK button on the properties sheet stores your entries and returns you to the desktop; clicking the Cancel button abandons your entries (retaining any previously set) and returns you to the desktop.

Date ...

```
┌─────────────────────────────────────────────┐
│ Date Series                                   │
│                                               │
│ Series Name:    ▐Series 3:03:42 AM▌           │
│ Category Name:  │H│                           │
│ Value Name:     │Y│                           │
│                                               │
│ First Category: │Jan 1, 1900│                 │
│ Increment Each Category By                    │
│ │1        │  ⊙ Years ○ Months ○ Days ○ Weekdays │
│                        [  OK  ] [ Cancel ]    │
└─────────────────────────────────────────────┘
```

The Date series type is similar to the Sequence series type; you enter only the value half of each data point, while Chart automatically provides a sequence of equally spaced dates as the category labels.

You can specify the beginning date, which Chart always presets to the current date kept by the system clock, in the First Category box. This date can be entered in almost any recognizable format. February 2, 1984, for example, can be entered as 2/2/84, 2 Feb 84, or February 2, 1984 (and probably in other formats I haven't discovered). If you manage to enter the date incorrectly, an alert box telling you the date format is invalid appears when you click the OK button.

If you leave the month or day out, the program sets them to 1; if you leave the year out, the program sets it to the current year kept by the system clock. The program computes the day of the week for you and provides it, if needed, in the series window and on the chart.

The first entry on the bottom line (Increment), determines the interval between dates in the series. You enter a number and then click the appropriate box to specify whether this increment is measured in years, months, days, or weekdays (Monday through Friday).

The program computes the dates and displays them in the format specified on the Categories Format properties sheet (which I will describe when we get to the Format menu).

Text ...

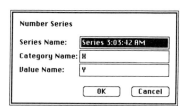

The properties sheet for a Text series is very short, asking only for the series, category, and value names. This type of series is used when you want to enter category labels such as Income, Expenses, or Profits in the left column of the series window, and numbers in the right column.

Number ...

The Number series, like the Text series, allows you to enter both columns in the series window; you have to fill in only the names on the properties sheet. This series type is useful for plotting scatter graphs, since it allows more than one value to be associated with a specific category.

Although you can change the series type after information has been entered, there are some restrictions imposed by the nature of each series. A text series, for example, when converted to another type (by selecting the series window and then choosing the new type from the Data menu), loses the text you entered in the category column. If you convert it to a sequence or date series, the text in the category column is replaced by Chart's entries, determined by the new properties sheet. If you convert it to a number series, the category column is filled with zeros, waiting for you to supply the new numbers. If you think about the nature of each series, the restrictions are rather obvious and easy to live with.

Sort ...

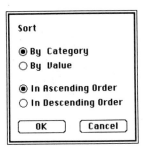

If you choose the Sort command with a series window selected, the selected series is rearranged in its window. A dialog box allows you to specify whether you would like the sort based on the category or the value column, and whether you would like the result arranged in ascending or descending order.

Since the sorted series replaces the original, if you think you will need the information presented in the original order again, make a copy of it before sorting.

Analyze ...

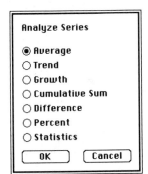

Choosing Analyze brings up this dialog box, which allows you to feed the data points in the selected series through a variety of formulas. The computed results are placed in another series window with a title indicating that it is the Average, Trend, or Growth of the selected series. The original series remains in its own series window and is not affected.

Average

Series 3:03:42 AM		Average of Series 3:03:42	
Order: 1		Order: 2	
⊠ Plot Series		⊠ Plot Series	
X	Y	X	Y
1	12	1	45
2	23	2	45
3	34	3	45
4	45	4	45
5	56	5	45
6	67	6	45
7	78	7	45

This display shows an original series and the result of computing its average. Although it may seem a little pointless to enter the same average on every line of the series window, doing so allows you to plot the average on the same chart as the original series, thereby illustrating when things were better than average and when they were worse.

Trend

Series 8:40:00 PM			Trend of Series 8:40:00 P	
Order: ▓▓▓			Order: ▓▓▓	
☐ Plot Series			☐ Plot Series	
X	Y		X	Y
1	12		1	17.571428571
2	34		2	26.542857143
3	21		3	35.514285714
4	54		4	44.485714286
5	76		5	53.457142857
6	43		6	62.428571429

Choosing Trend creates a new series that is the linear regression of the selected series.

Growth

Series 8:40:00 PM			Growth of Series 8:40:00	
Order: ▓▓▓			Order: ▓▓▓	
☐ Plot Series			☐ Plot Series	
X	Y		X	Y
1	12		1	16.897036936
2	34		2	22.318072450
3	21		3	29.478325685
4	54		4	38.935785656
5	76		5	51.427459648
6	43		6	67.926807210

The series created by the Growth command has values that correspond to a fitted exponential curve approximation of the original series.

Cumulative Sum

Series 8:40:00 PM			Cumulative sum of Series	
Order: ▓▓▓			Order: ▓▓▓	
☐ Plot Series			☐ Plot Series	
X	Y		X	Y
1	12		1	12
2	34		2	46
3	21		3	67
4	54		4	121
5	76		5	197
6	43		6	240

To create a Cumulative Sum series, each value in the original series is added to the sum of all previous values. The first value in a Cumulative Sum series is always equal to the first value of the original series, the second value is equal to the sum of the first two in the original series, and so on.

Difference

Series 8:40:00 PM		Differences of Series 8:4	
Order:		Order:	
□ Plot Series		□ Plot Series	
X	Y	X	Y
1	12	1	12
2	34	2	22
3	21	3	-13
4	54	4	33
5	76	5	22
6	43	6	-33

To create a Difference series, each value in the original series is subtracted from the value on the line above it. This formula is handy for plotting the difference in something, such as profits, over a period of time.

Percent

Series 8:40:00 PM		Percentages of Series 8:4	
Order:		Order:	
□ Plot Series		□ Plot Series	
X	Y	X	Y
1	12	1	5%
2	34	2	14%
3	21	3	9%
4	54	4	23%
5	76	5	32%
6	43	6	18%

Each line in a Percent series shows what percentage that line contributed to the total of the original series.

Statistics

Series 8:40:00 PM		Statistics on Series 8:40:	
Order:		Order:	
□ Plot Series		□ Plot Series	
X	Y	X	Y
1	12	# of points	6
2	34	Maximum	76
3	21	Minimum	12
4	54	Average	40
5	76	Median	43
6	43	Std. Deviati	23.160310879
		Corr. Coeff.	0.7246882859

The Statistics series window displays several pieces of information about the original series; the most significant are the standard deviation and the correlation coefficient, both useful in analyzing scatter graphs.

List ...

Choosing the List command produces this dialog box, which lists each series you have created or brought into the program during this session. The two check boxes in front of each series name allow you to open or close that series window (Show) and specify whether or not it will be included in the current chart (Plot). Clicking in a box toggles an X on or off in the box; if the box in the first column (Show) has an X in it, the series window is open and on your desktop, though it may be buried. If the box in the second column (Plot) is X'ed, the series is plotted on the chart.

The Gallery Menu

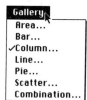

The Gallery menu is simply a list of the different graph formats supported by Chart. The check mark (presently in front of Column Chart) indicates the format in which your data will be plotted. The program is preset to the column chart format, but you can choose another format by moving the highlight and releasing the mouse button.

When you choose a format, a display of Chart's standard versions of that format appears on your screen. When you select a specific version by clicking it, your data is plotted in that version of that format. Each of the next six chapters deals with one of these formats.

The Chart Menu

You use commands from the Chart menu to designate all or part of the chart for further action or to set properties that apply to the chart.

Main Chart Type ...

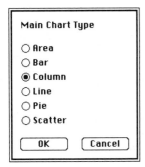

The dialog box for Main Chart Type gives you another way to set the chart format, which you do by clicking the desired type or the circle to its left.

Main Chart Type is used in conjunction with Main Chart (from the Format menu) to individually set many of the parameters that are automatically set when you choose a predefined format from one of the galleries. This is a useful technique for when no predefined combination of parameters exactly matches your desires.

Overlay Chart Type ...

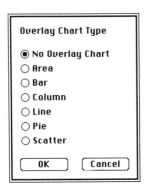

In addition to plotting multiple series on the same chart you can place one chart on top of another. This is done to produce charts in combinations of formats, such as column and line, or charts with multiple value axes. The chart you place on top is called an overlay, and choosing Overlay Chart Type from the Chart menu allows you to select a type or to specify that there will be no overlay chart, in case you already have one. If you eliminate an existing overlay, then the series that were plotted on it are instead included in the main chart.

If you have decided to use the overlay feature and are plotting more than two series, the program automatically distributes the series as evenly as possible between the main chart and the overlay. You can control which series goes where by editing the order box in each series window—the lower half of the order range is plotted on the main chart and the upper half on the overlay chart. (You can also control the series distribution to some degree in the dialog box displayed when you chose Overlay Chart from the Format menu.)

Axes ...

```
Axes

For Categories Show        For Values Show
☒ Axis                     ☒ Axis
☒ Tick Mark Labels         ☒ Tick Mark Labels
☐ Major Grid Lines         ☐ Major Grid Lines
☐ Minor Grid Lines         ☐ Minor Grid Lines

                    [   OK   ]   [ Cancel ]
```

By selecting options in the Chart Axes dialog box, you can turn various visual attributes of the chart on and off. An X in a check box indicates the attribute will be visible, an empty box indicates it will not. The pattern used to display each of the visible attributes can be set from the Format menu.

Add Legend

Choosing Add Legend displays on the chart a key composed of each series title and a sample of its pattern. When chosen, this menu item changes to Delete Legend; choosing Delete Legend reverses the process.

Add Arrow

The Add Arrow command becomes available (printed in black) after you have created an insertion box on the chart. I explained briefly how to do this in Chapter 2, but in case you've forgotten, I'll go over it again.

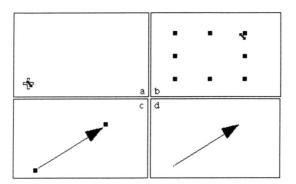

To create an insertion box, position the pointer where you would like the end of the arrow's shaft to start and press the mouse button; the pointer changes to a white cross with a double-headed arrow diagonally through it. Keeping the mouse button pressed, drag the cross to where you would like the arrow's point to appear. An insertion box surrounded by black squares (called handles) is formed immediately when you release the mouse button.

When you choose Add Arrow, an arrow is drawn diagonally across the box. The arrow has a black handle at each end to indicate that it is selected; selecting something else removes these handles.

You can move the arrow or change its size and the direction it points by first selecting it and then dragging one of the handles. Get rid of an unwanted arrow by first selecting it and then choosing Clear from the Edit menu. Other arrow properties can be set by selecting the arrow and then choosing Patterns from the Format menu.

Select Chart

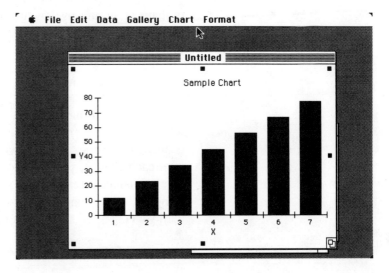

You use the Select Chart command to mark the entire chart for some action—moving it, framing it, or changing its size, for example. The fact that you have selected the chart is indicated by the appearance of little black handles around it.

Select Plot Area

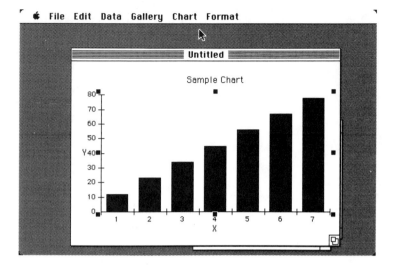

The Select Plot Area command is comparable to the Select Chart command, except it only marks the plot area. Once a plot area is selected, you can use the mouse to change the size or shape of the area by dragging the handles, and you can use the Pattern command from the Format menu to change the background and border patterns.

Redraw Now

If you have chosen the Manual Redraw command, which I'll discuss in a moment, in order to make multiple changes to a series window without the chart being updated after each change, you can choose Redraw Now to see the effects of your changes. You can also click in the chart window to bring it to the surface, which causes the chart to be redrawn with your changes but leaves it in the Manual Redraw mode.

Automatic Redraw

This command is preset by the program, and you normally leave it that way. With Automatic Redraw set, every time you modify the chart or change the information in a plotted series window, the chart is redrawn to reflect the change.

Manual Redraw

Manual Redraw is the alternative to Automatic Redraw. When you choose the Manual Redraw command, the chart is erased, precluding any direct changes. This allows you to rearrange series windows and change the values in them without waiting for the chart to be redrawn between each change. To see how things are going, you can choose Redraw Now from time to time, or wait until you have made all your changes and then choose Automatic Redraw. (The chart is also redrawn if you bring the chart window to the surface by selecting it.)

Show Chart Window

Moving the pointer to Show Chart Window and releasing the mouse button brings the chart window to the top of the stack of windows on your desktop. You can accomplish the same end by simply clicking anyplace in the chart window, and this second method is usually faster. The only time this command is really useful is when you have made the chart window very small and then lost it in the clutter.

The Format Menu

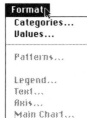

Format commands can be applied to parts and properties of the chart—such as an axis, a legend, a piece of text, or a segment of a bar. If you first select a specific item and then pull down the Format menu, the commands applicable to your selected item are printed in black. The actual dialog box that is presented when you choose one of these commands is determined by the specific object selected at that moment.

For example, choosing Patterns produces different dialog boxes, depending on whether you have an axis, an arrow, or some other chart object selected.

When you create a chart, the program automatically makes format decisions based on standards that apply to the type of chart you are creating. You can choose commands from this menu if you want to override these decisions while customizing a chart or creating a special effect.

Categories ...

```
Categories

Align              Show
○ Left             ⊠ Year
○ Center           □ Quarter
◉ Right            ⊠ Month
                   □ Day
Date Format        □ Day of Week
○ Short
◉ Medium
○ Long

Text Before: [                ]
Text After:  [                ]

        [   OK   ]  [ Cancel ]
```

The Categories command is only available (printed in black) when a series window is selected. The format in which information is displayed both in the left column of the selected series window and on the chart, can be defined in a Categories dialog box. Choosing Categories allows you to specify three things: how the text will be aligned in the category column; the format, in both the column and on the chart, of any numbers or dates used as category labels; and the automatic insertion on the chart of specified text before or after the labels. The information in the Categories dialog box varies slightly with the type of series selected (sequence, date, and so on). For example, the Categories dialog box presented when a date series is selected allows you to specify the date format as well as the alignment, number format, and text before and after.

Values ...

The Values command is also available only when a series window is selected. Choosing this command allows you to control the appearance of the numbers in the value column of the series window and on the chart. The dialog box for Values is identical to that for Categories (with the exception of the unnecessary ability to set date formats).

Patterns ...

One of nine different dialog boxes appears when you choose Patterns from the Format menu. As I have already mentioned, the dialog box you are presented with is determined by the object you select on the chart before you choose Patterns.

Background and border patterns

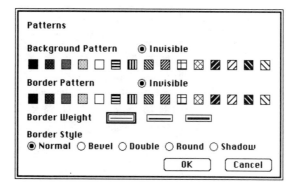

If you select the entire chart (by choosing Select Chart from the Chart menu), the legend, or a piece of text, this is the dialog box that appears when you choose Patterns from the Format menu.

The background and the border can be individually set to any one of fifteen visible patterns, or each can be made invisible. If you make the border visible, then you can also set its weight and style.

If only the plot area, rather than the entire chart, is selected, the Patterns dialog box differs only in that you cannot set the border style—it is preset to one style.

Axis patterns

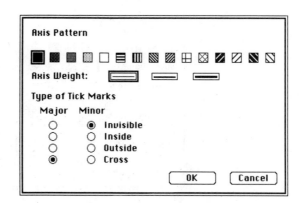

Selecting one of the axes before you choose Patterns produces this dialog box. In addition to setting the axis-line pattern and weight, you can specify whether the program should display major and minor tick marks (indicating axis divisions), and if so, their style.

Segment patterns

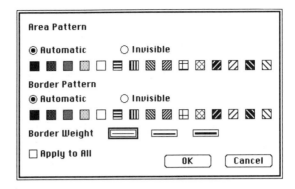

This dialog box is the result of selecting a segment of a bar, column, pie, or area chart before choosing Patterns. Two significant items in this dialog box are the Apply to All Areas check box and the Automatic button.

Clicking Apply to All Areas causes your pattern selections to be applied to all segments of a selected series.

Automatic is the preset selection for Area Pattern, and allows the chart program to select and distribute patterns in its own logical manner. When multiple patterns are used, Chart arranges them in the order they appear in this dialog box.

Arrow patterns

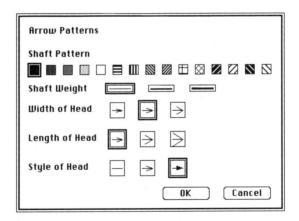

The Arrow Patterns dialog box allows you to set the pattern and weight of an arrow, and the width, length, and style of its head. As with the other dialog boxes, the specifications set in this one apply only to the specific object selected on the chart at the time you chose Patterns. You can have dozens of arrows on your chart, each with different properties.

Grid patterns

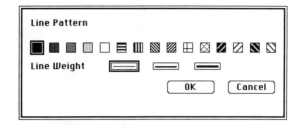

Selecting a horizontal or vertical grid line and then choosing Patterns produces this dialog box, allowing you to set the pattern and weight that are applied to all grid lines of the same type—major horizontal, minor vertical, and so on.

Line patterns

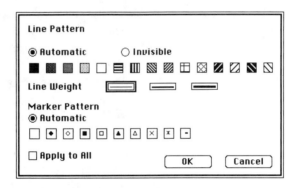

Selecting either a segment of one of the lines on a multi-series line chart, or a marker on that line, before choosing Patterns, brings up this dialog box. The Automatic buttons, for both the line and marker patterns, cause patterns to be distributed automatically among multiple lines on a chart.

You can use the markers to differentiate the data points in line and scatter graphs. Clicking Apply to All, applies your pattern, weight, and marker choices to all lines and points plotted on the chart.

If you only have one series plotted on your line graph, you can set each line segment or marker by selecting it and choosing Patterns from the Format menu. Different dialog boxes appear for line and marker, but the combination of choices in these two boxes is the same as in the dialog box for a multi-series line graph.

Legend ...

```
┌──────────────────────────────────────────────┐
│  Legend                                        │
│                                                │
│  Font                          Font Size       │
│  ⦿ Geneva      ☐ Italic        ⦿ Small         │
│  ○ New York    ☐ Bold          ○ Medium        │
│  ○ Chicago                     ○ Large         │
│                                                │
│  Type of       Automatic       Spacing of      │
│  Legend                        Entries         │
│  ○ Bottom      ☒ Size          ⦿ Close         │
│  ○ Corner      ☒ Position      ○ Medium        │
│  ○ Top                         ○ Open          │
│  ⦿ Vertical                                    │
│                                                │
│               ┌────────┐     ┌──────────┐      │
│               │   OK   │     │  Cancel  │      │
│               └────────┘     └──────────┘      │
└──────────────────────────────────────────────┘
```

If you have already ordered a legend for your chart (by choosing Add Legend from the Chart menu), you can control its appearance by choosing Legend from the Format menu. As with the other Format commands, you must first select the object you would like to format (in this case the legend) before you can choose the command.

The Font, Font Size, Italic, and Bold selections at the top of the dialog box control the appearance of the letters in the legend labels.

The selections in the bottom part of the box determine the location and appearance of the legend; Vertical, the preset selection, places it along the right side of the chart. Spacing refers to the amount of space between the legend's components, and therefore controls its overall size. If you move the legend or change its size (by dragging with the mouse), and want to return it to its preset conditions, choose Add Legend again and click the Automatic boxes in this dialog box.

Text ...

Each piece of selectable text on the chart has a properties sheet associated with it. You normally have no need to alter the preset conditions on this sheet, but if you want to, you can control many attributes.

There are a lot of selections to choose from in this dialog box; for the purpose of explanation I will divide them into groups of related choices and highlight each group in the illustration as it is discussed.

```
┌─────────────────────────────────────────────────────────────────────┐
│ Text                                                                  │
│                                                                       │
│ Font                     Font Size      Automatic     Show            │
│ ◉ Geneva     ☐ Italic    ○ Small        ☒ Text        ☐ Key           │
│ ○ New York   ☐ Bold      ◉ Medium       ☒ Size        ☐ Value         │
│ ○ Chicago                ○ Large                                      │
│                                                                       │
│ Attached To              Orientation    Horizontal    Vertical        │
│ ○ Unattached             ◉ Horizontal   Alignment     Alignment       │
│ ○ Chart Title            ○ Vertical     ○ Left        ○ Top           │
│ ○ Category Axis                         ◉ Center      ◉ Center        │
│ ◉ Value Axis                            ○ Right       ○ Bottom        │
│ ○ Series or Data Point                                               │
│                                                                       │
│ Series Number: [                ]                                     │
│                                     ┌────────┐   ┌──────────┐        │
│ Point Number:  [                ]   │   OK   │   │  Cancel  │        │
│                                     └────────┘   └──────────┘        │
└─────────────────────────────────────────────────────────────────────┘
```

The font selections, orientation, and alignment control the placement and appearance of the selected text, with alignment referring to the placement of the text within the frame (usually invisible) surrounding it.

```
┌─────────────────────────────────────────────────────────────────────┐
│ Text                                                                  │
│                                                                       │
│ Font                     Font Size      Automatic     Show            │
│ ◉ Geneva     ☐ Italic    ○ Small        ☒ Text        ☐ Key           │
│ ○ New York   ☐ Bold      ◉ Medium       ☒ Size        ☐ Value         │
│ ○ Chicago                ○ Large                                      │
│                                                                       │
│ Attached To              Orientation    Horizontal    Vertical        │
│ ○ Unattached             ◉ Horizontal   Alignment     Alignment       │
│ ○ Chart Title            ○ Vertical     ○ Left        ○ Top           │
│ ○ Category Axis                         ◉ Center      ◉ Center        │
│ ◉ Value Axis                            ○ Right       ○ Bottom        │
│ ○ Series or Data Point                                               │
│                                                                       │
│ Series Number: [                ]                                     │
│                                     ┌────────┐   ┌──────────┐        │
│ Point Number:  [                ]   │   OK   │   │  Cancel  │        │
│                                     └────────┘   └──────────┘        │
└─────────────────────────────────────────────────────────────────────┘
```

This section of the Text properties sheet deals with whether the selected text is attached to another chart object, and if so, which one. Using this section you can attach text to the chart title, one of the axes, or a segment on the chart.

There is an advantage and a disadvantage to being attached. The advantage is that, if you change the size or location of the chart, the text moves with the object it is attached to. The disadvantage is that you are restricted in the directions you can move attached text relative to the object it is attached to. For example, if you attach text to one of the columns in a column chart, and then change the chart to a pie chart, the attached text appears beside the same segment in the pie chart that it was above in the column chart. Had the text been unattached when you changed chart type, it would have stayed exactly where it was in the chart window.

If you attach text to a segment, you have to fill in the two boxes marked Series Number and Point Number. The series number is the number that appears in the order box in the series window, and the point number is the line in the series window value column that contains the plotted point to which you want to attach the text.

```
┌─────────────────────────────────────────────────────────────┐
│ Text                                                          │
│                                                               │
│ Font                    Font Size      Automatic    Show      │
│ ◉ Geneva    ☐ Italic    ○ Small        ☒ Text       ☐ Key     │
│ ○ New York  ☐ Bold      ◉ Medium       ☒ Size       ☐ Value   │
│ ○ Chicago               ○ Large                               │
│                                                               │
│ Attached To             Orientation    Horizontal   Vertical  │
│ ○ Unattached            ◉ Horizontal   Alignment    Alignment │
│ ○ Chart Title           ○ Vertical     ○ Left        ○ Top     │
│ ○ Category Axis                        ◉ Center     ◉ Center   │
│ ◉ Value Axis                           ○ Right      ○ Bottom   │
│ ○ Series or Data Point                                        │
│ Series Number: [            ]                                 │
│ Point Number:  [            ]       ( OK )    ( Cancel )       │
└─────────────────────────────────────────────────────────────┘
```

The Automatic Text click box controls the source of certain text, such as the chart title and the axis labels. If there is an X in this box, the Chart program provided the text you presently have selected. If you edit the text, replacing it with your own, the X goes away. If you would like to return to the automatically provided text, simply click the Automatic Text box.

If Automatic Size is selected, the insertion frame, created to hold the text entered on the chart, expands to display as much text as is entered. If this option is not selected, you have to drag the handles on the frame to enlarge it, if necessary.

The Show Key and Show Value options apply to text that has been attached to a series or a data point. Clicking Key displays with the text a small swatch of the pattern associated with the series or the point that the text is attached to.

Clicking Value causes the attached text to be replaced with a number representing the value of the data point it is attached to. This number is taken from the series window, so it is as accurate as the number you entered.

Axis (Main Chart or Overlay Chart) ...

There are two Axis properties sheets, one for the category axis and one for the value axis. If you have plotted an overlay chart, and select an axis, the axis entry in the Format menu will indicate that you have selected either a Main Chart Axis or an Overlay Chart Axis. As with other properties, Chart automatically makes the best selections on these properties sheets for the chart you are producing. You only have to alter the preset selections if you want to customize the chart.

An option that is common to all axis properties sheets is that of setting the tick label position. The three choices—Low, High, and Next to Axis—appear near the bottom of the dialog box. The Low and High options place the tick labels below the lowest plotted point or above the highest plotted point on the chart; this is useful with deviation charts that extend below and above the zero line. The Next to Axis option is preselected and is most often the correct choice.

Category axis

```
┌─────────────────────────────────────────────────────┐
│ ┌───────────────────────────────────────────────┐   │
│ │ Category Axis                                   │   │
│ │ Value Axis Crosses                              │   │
│ │   at Category Number:        [1          ]     │   │
│ │ Number of Categories                            │   │
│ │   Between Tick Mark Labels:  [1       ]        │   │
│ │                                                 │   │
│ │ ☐ Value Axis Crosses Between Categories         │   │
│ │ ☐ Categories in Reverse Order                   │   │
│ │                                                 │   │
│ │ Tick Label Position                             │   │
│ │ ○ Low   ○ High  ◉ Next to Axis                  │   │
│ │                   [   OK   ]   [ Cancel ]       │   │
│ └───────────────────────────────────────────────┘   │
└─────────────────────────────────────────────────────┘
```

This is the properties sheet for the category axis, except when you are plotting a scatter graph, in which case the properties sheet is identical to the Value Axis properties sheet. The category axis is the horizontal axis on most charts (but the vertical axis on bar charts).

At the top of this dialog box you can specify at what point the other axis is to cross this one. The crossing point is preset to the first category, which produces the normal axes you can see in the chart window behind the dialog box. The most common alternative is to click Categories in Reverse Order, which causes the value axis to cross at the opposite end of the category axis. This option is useful when plotting overlay charts with different value scales; one scale can be at one side of the chart and the other scale at the other side.

You can also specify on this properties sheet whether the value axis crosses on or between data points; if it crosses between points there is some space between the value axis and the first plotted point—a desirable attribute in bar and column charts but not in area and line charts.

Another option you can specify is the number of categories between labels. The initial setting of 1 will force a label on every category. If you have long labels or many categories, you can increase the setting to reduce the number of labels.

Value axis

The properties sheet for the value axis (also for the category axis for scatter graphs) has a few more items on it than the one for the category axis, but they are very straightforward. The Minimum, Maximum, Major Unit, and Minor Unit settings refer to the values of the tick marks on the axis. The major units are the increments between major tick marks and the minor units are the increments between minor tick marks. In most cases only the major tick marks are displayed (you determine what is displayed in the Axis Patterns dialog box).

The minimum tick-mark value is automatically set at zero if all plotted values are positive; otherwise it is set at the next major unit below the lowest number. The maximum tick-mark value is set at the next major unit above the highest number—or zero if all numbers are negative.

The category axis normally crosses the value axis at zero, but this too can be changed for special effects, such as an indexed chart or a floating column chart (both discussed later). Clicking Values in Reverse Order causes the vertical axis scales to reverse, with positive numbers descending from the horizontal axis, and negative ones ascending.

Clicking Logarithmic Scale converts the normal arithmetic scale to logarithmic values, which is convenient for displaying data points that span a great range of values.

Main Chart . . .

The properties sheet presented when you choose Main Chart is determined by the type of chart you are working with; each type has a sheet containing selections specific to it. As with other properties sheets, these are preset to the most commonly used values. You can easily change the preset conditions by editing this sheet or by choosing another chart variation from the Gallery menu.

Value Axis

Range		Automatic
Minimum	0	☒
Maximum	90	☒
Major Unit:	10	☒
Minor Unit:	2	☒
Category Axis Crosses At:	0	☒

☐ Logarithmic Scale
☐ Values In Reverse Order

Tick Label Position
○ Low ○ High ◉ Next to Axis

[OK] [Cancel]

All Main Chart properties sheets have click boxes to allow the program to set the chart size and position and the plot-area size and position automatically. If you manually move the chart or change its size and then decide you would prefer things the way they were, click these boxes to return control to the program. Each properties sheet also has an OK and a Cancel button. After you have selected changes you would like to make, click the OK button to put them into effect. If you change your mind and decide to leave things the way they are, click the Cancel button to return all options to their previous conditions. Either way, you are returned to the Chart desktop.

Area Chart

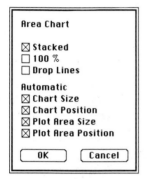

The Area Chart properties sheet allows you to set the manner in which multiple series are displayed (Stacked and 100%) and whether there will be Drop Lines. Technically, all area charts are stacked; if you change this parameter, what you have is no longer an area chart, it's a filled line chart or a band chart. Changing this parameter can be a useful, but potentially deceptive, technique for special effects. You should read the information about Area Charts in Chapter 9 before using this properties sheet to change any of the parameters automatically set by the Chart program.

Bar Chart

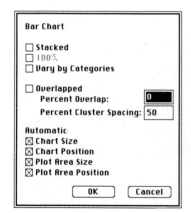

On the Bar and Column Chart properties sheets, Stacked, 100%, and Overlapped pertain to charts with more than one series. If you click Stacked, the bars that were clustered together side by side are laid out so the beginning of one is aligned with the end of the previous one, in a step format. Normally, stacked bars are also overlapped, so they appear to be one continuous bar divided into segments. If you click 100%, the segmented bars are stretched to fill the width (bar) or height (column) of the chart, with the length of each segment representing that segment's share of the bar's total value.

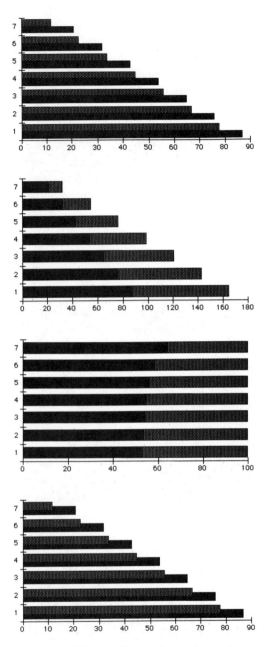

These illustrations show the same multiple-series bar chart plotted in the standard, the stacked, the 100-percent stacked, and the overlapped formats. The amount of overlap is specified on the properties sheet as a percentage of the width of one bar, as is the spacing between clusters of bars. When you change from one format to another, the Chart program automatically adjusts the value scale.

The Vary by Categories option, which appears in the Bar, Column, and Pie Chart dialog boxes, applies to charts with only one series; clicking it causes each bar in the series to be shaded with a different pattern, up to fifteen patterns, after which Chart starts repeating.

Column Chart

With the exception of its title, the Column Chart properties sheet is identical to the one just described for the bar chart. Each option controls the same parameters; everything is just rotated 90 degrees.

Line Chart

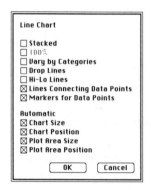

The Line Chart properties sheet allows you to produce both a stacked and a 100-percent stacked line chart, which are really the same as area charts without the areas filled in.

Vary by Categories applies only to charts displaying just one series, and controls the distribution of patterns used as markers for each data point.

You can add Hi-Lo lines, extending from the highest to the lowest series at each category, and Drop Lines, which go from the highest series to the horizontal axis. You will see examples of how these lines are used in Chapter 7. By clicking Lines Connecting Data Points and Markers for Data Points, you can make each of these attributes disappear and reappear.

Pie Chart

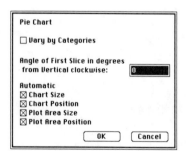

The Pie Chart properties sheet has only two extra options: Vary by Categories and Angle of First Slice. Choosing Vary by Categories causes each pie segment to have a different pattern, just as it did with the bar and column charts. The first-slice angle is set in degrees of clockwise rotation from the top point of the circle (the preset 0-degree starting point).

Scatter Chart

The Scatter Chart properties sheet allows you to turn lines and points on and off—although if you turned both off there wouldn't be much left to look at.

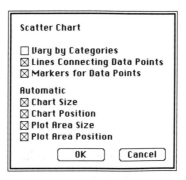

Overlay Chart . . .

The six properties sheets available when you choose Overlay Chart have most of the same options to select from as their counterparts from Main Chart. Which one of the six comes up is determined by the type of overlay chart plotted.

These properties sheets do not have automatic size and position selections; these features are controlled from the Main Chart properties sheet for both the main and overlay chart. There are, however, two new items that are standard on all overlay chart properties sheets.

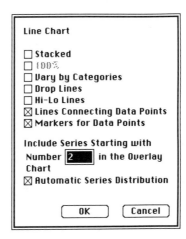

You can specify the order number of the series that the overlay will start with—that series and all above it in order will appear on the overlay chart—or you can click Automatic Series Distribution to allow the program to distribute the series between the main and overlay charts.

With automatic distribution, the series with low order numbers are plotted on the main chart and the series with high order numbers on the overlay. The split is determined by dividing the total number of series to be plotted by two and rounding an uneven result to the next highest number. If, for example, there are ten series, the first five go on the main chart and the last five on the overlay. If there are eleven, the first six go on the main chart and the last five on the overlay.

The End of the Tour

The accessibility through the menu bar of all Chart's commands and options makes it very easy for you to experiment with them. I encourage you to do so. There is no possibility of doing harm to the program or to the Macintosh by messing around. If things get hopelessly out of control and you can't seem to untangle the mess, remember that you can choose New from the File menu: If the chart window is on top, all format changes you have made return to Chart's preset conditions; if the series window is on top, all data is cleared.

As you continue with this book, you will be shown how to use each command to create and modify charts. If you forget what a command does, and would rather read about it than try it out, return to this section to refresh your memory.

5

The Column Chart

The column chart is a standard choice for showing the value of an item as it varies at precise intervals over a period of time (as with a budget that is set once a year or income that is totaled at the end of every month).

In the first part of this chapter, I will introduce the standards you should keep in mind when you are either creating a simple column chart or converting from a simple variation to a slightly more sophisticated one. The remainder of the chapter will be devoted to using Microsoft Chart on the Macintosh to produce column charts and to prepare them for presentation.

Standards

Unless you have specified otherwise, the Chart program automatically generates a simple column chart, such as the one you created in Chapter 2. You can then modify this chart either by choosing a variation from the Gallery menu or by changing individual components. If neither of these possibilities produces the chart you want, you can switch to another format: area, bar, line, scatter, pie, or some combination of these.

Each format provides a basic gallery of charts: This is the Column Chart Gallery.

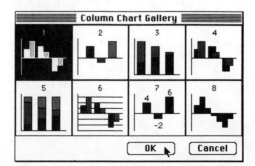

You can select the chart that most closely resembles the manner in which you would like to display your numeric values and then modify and personalize it to more precisely express your point of view.

The Simple Column Chart

The simple column chart is a readily accepted and easily interpreted format. It is not considered as technical as line and scatter graphs, and is not, therefore, as threatening to the nontechnical audience.

In the column format, the height of the column above the base line (usually zero) corresponds to the value of an item at one specific time. The units of time are shown along the chart's horizontal (category) axis, and the values, either in absolute units (such as dollars or gallons) or as a percentage of a total, are shown along the vertical (value) axis.

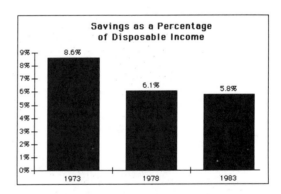

Placement of columns

Your column chart can take on a variety of aspects, depending on the number of time periods covered and the number of items compared for each period. The columns, for example, can be separate from each other, shoved together into one group, or arranged in sets of two or more. If separate, the columns should be wider than the spaces between them.

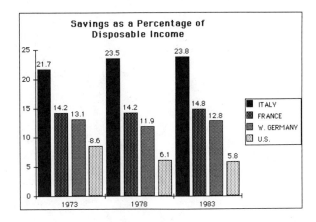

When you have plotted enough columns to cause crowding, simply eliminate the spaces between them to create a connected column chart.

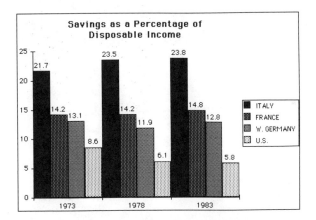

If you get to the point where you have too many columns to fit across the page, switch to a line graph; or rotate the axes 90 degrees and present your information horizontally as a bar chart. (This rotation is considered unorthodox by some, as it violates the rule of using a column chart to show variations in an item over a period of time; but every rule has an exception.)

If you are plotting more than one series over the same time period, consider grouping the columns representing the different items for each interval. Grouping allows you to make comparisons easily—both within and between the series.

When you use this format, try to limit the number of series to four so as not to clutter the chart and confuse the reader.

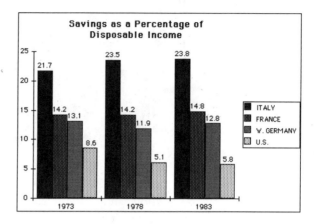

The separation between groups of two should be about the width of one column; groups of three or four require a column-and-a-half. However, to achieve balance or to help squeeze more information onto the chart, you can reduce the space between the columns in each group, place them directly against each other, or overlap them. The latter option looks best when the columns in each group can be arranged in order of descending height, so the overlapping columns are shorter than the ones beneath them. This arrangement avoids the "skinny" columns seen in this chart.

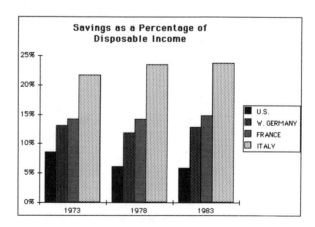

Shading and patterns

Shading and patterns can be used to attract attention, to add interest, to emphasize a point, or to differentiate between segments.

Generally, it is not necessary, or even appropriate, to use a variety of shades or patterns on a simple column chart; but if you have a reason for doing so, it is considered good practice to order the shades from dark to light and to place the darkest shade nearest the value axis.

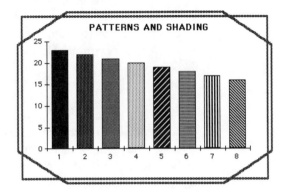

With grouped columns, shading is used to differentiate and identify the series. If the purpose of your graph is to prove a point or influence a decision, bear in mind that a darker column tends to stand out, appearing larger, closer, and more important than a lighter column of the same size.

Select patterns carefully. Although your choices won't make a poorly designed chart interesting and informative, they certainly can detract from an otherwise well-designed chart and may prevent people from taking it seriously. The wrong combination of patterns can create optical illusions that make the most carefully drawn lines appear crooked.

Labels

There is adequate room for artistic expression in the design of a graphic display. Your striking arrangement of shapes and patterns may be the factor that determines whether your chart is read rather than rejected. However, when it comes to labels you should control your creative efforts. Once the chart has attracted attention, the primary objective is to pass the maximum amount of information in the minimum amount of time. There should be no room for confusion or misunderstanding in your presentation of labels or numbers. The ultimate purpose of the chart is, after all, to get those numbers across to your audience, not to demonstrate your ability to turn dry, statistical information into an exotic art form.

Titles and labels should be short and descriptive; if you are charting sex in the suburbs, then the title of your chart is *Sex in the Suburbs,* not *Courting and Reproductive Rituals Practiced in Outlying Residential Communities.* Try to keep everything short enough to be printed on one line.

Having a multitude of fancy fonts and type sizes available doesn't mean you have to use them all on the same chart. Stick to the same type style throughout, with numbers and letters of compatible style and size.

Axes

The scales that your short, pithy, horizontal labels describe should be chosen for easy interpretation and interpolation. The reader should be able to guess the values between and beyond the printed numbers accurately. If the distance between numbers makes judging the intermediate values difficult, partition the value axis with tick marks and carry the scale values across to the columns with grid lines.

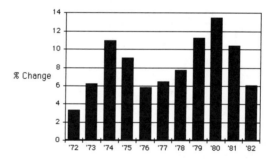

Start measurements from zero whenever possible. If you have to start higher due to the magnitude of the measurements, make it obvious that you have done so.

The value scale can be placed at the left or right side of the chart, or, in the case of wide charts, at both sides.

Legends

When a legend (also called a key), is appropriate to relate labels to patterns, Chart provides one at your request.

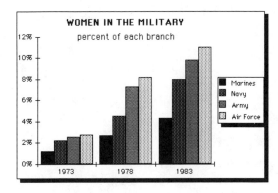

The legend can be set off with a frame and placed within the chart to balance any lopsidedness, or it can run along the top or bottom of the chart. If you decide to use some other method to identify each series (such as a label and arrow), you can delete the legend.

Most of the numeric relationships you will have occasion to work with can probably be expressed adequately with simple column charts, such as those you have seen so far in this chapter. There are, however, other variations available. One popular style is the stacked column chart, which is selection number 3 from the Column Chart Gallery you saw at the beginning of this chapter.

The Stacked Column Chart

The stacked column chart is an alternative to the grouped column chart, placing each series on top of the one previously charted, instead of by its side. The height of the resulting column indicates the sum of the individual series values.

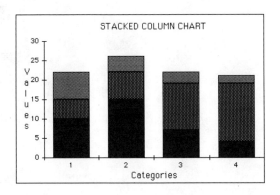

This cumulative effect can be seen on the chart shown here. In the first column, the bottom segment, which has a value of 10, extends upward to that level on the Y-axis. The second segment, which has a value of 5, starts at the 10 level and continues to 15, which is the sum of the two. The third segment adds its value, 7, to the previous two, and continues on up to 22.

Plotting your information in the stacked-column format allows an easy visual comparison of the amount that each segment contributes to the whole. If you would like to stress this relationship, you can scale the value axis in percentages rather than in actual values.

Shading

Shading is particularly important on the stacked column chart. The darkest shade should be on the bottom, with the segments becoming progressively lighter toward the top. Since the segment that is plotted nearest the base line is the easiest to interpret, that spot should be reserved, if possible, for the series you want to emphasize.

The 100-Percent Stacked Column Chart

If the stacked columns are reformed to extend from the 0-percent line to the 100-percent line and the segments of each column are shown as portions of the whole, the format, which looks similar to this, is called a 100-percent stacked column chart. Although the precise numerical values of items expressed in this manner are difficult to interpret, their relationship to the whole is more obvious.

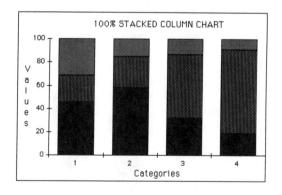

The Deviation Column Chart

Usually we think of a graph as extending in a positive direction from the zero base line. However, as you saw in the

Column Chart Gallery, this isn't always the case. With Chart, if you enter negative values for one or more categories in the series window, the program automatically moves the zero base line up the vertical axis and extend the columns up and down from it, as appropriate. This deviation column chart shows profits and losses of a hypothetical business.

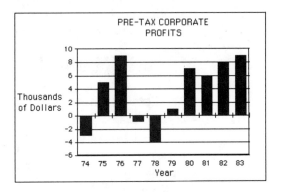

The Range Column Chart

The series of column segments shown here represents the normal range of temperatures in Seattle, based on the average temperature over a 30-year period. This is a typical application of the range column chart.

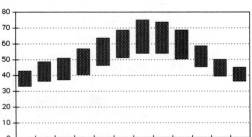

Though this variation of the column chart is similar in style to the high-low format available from the Line Chart Gallery, it requires a little extra manipulation to create.

All the rules for labeling and shading other column charts apply to this one as well. The primary difference between this and other column charts is that the columns don't start at the zero base line, but at the low point for their particular category. The low-to-high range of the column, measured against the value axis, represents the range of the item during the time period represented on the category axis.

The Floating Column Chart

In a floating column chart, each column is divided into two major components, each of which can be further subdivided. One component extends upward from the zero base line; the other extends downward directly beneath the first.

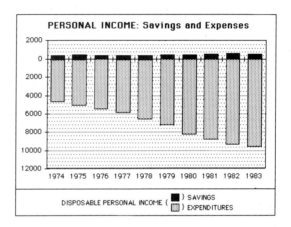

This floating column chart shows a breakdown of the average disposable personal income and expenditures for U.S. citizens from 1974 to 1983. The total range of each column is a measure of the net disposable income for that year. The segments below the zero line represent what was spent; the little bit that peeks over the top is what was theoretically saved. Unlike the deviation column chart, the scale is positive both above and below the zero line.

Creating Column Charts

Now that you are familiar with the various column charts and the standards that apply to them, let's create a few. In the next sections I will lead you through the steps involved in creating a simple column chart, adding more information to it, and converting it to the variations we have just discussed.

The Simple Column Chart

The information for this first example, as for most of the examples in this chapter, is taken from the 1982-83 edition of the *Statistical Abstract of the United States*, an interesting book of numbers published by the Government Printing Office.

Suppose you want to analyze the annual income and expenses required to run this country from 1940 to 1980. The purpose of this chart (I did say that the first step in creating a chart was determining the purpose) is to compare the change in government spending to the corresponding change in income over this 40-year period.

After analyzing the available information, you decide that a column chart would be an appropriate format—there are less than a dozen data points in the series (nine), they vary over time (the primary prerequisite), and they can be measured at precise intervals (you will plot every fifth year).

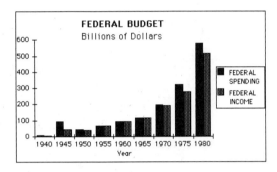

Your finished chart will resemble this one. The steps in creating a chart were explained in Chapter 2, and the meaning of each command in the Chart program was explained in Chapter 4. I will assume you have either read these chapters or otherwise managed to master the methods of data entry and editing, so I can dispense with some of the details here.

Getting ready

If you have been working on another chart, the first step in creating a new one is cleaning up the desktop. Save your old chart (if you would like to return to it later) and clear the screen by twice choosing New from the File menu—once with the chart window selected and once with a series window selected—to clear both the format changes you have made and the data you have entered. You should have nothing left in front of you but empty windows.

Creating the series

You will first create a series to show spending, then another to show income. To create this series you could simply select the New Series window and start typing values. Chart would produce a sequence series and title it with the current time. Your values would appear in the right column of the series window—opposite a sequence of numbers supplied by Chart. The series type and name could be changed later.

But since you already know the type and titles you want, let's enter them right at the start. Choose Date from the Data menu and a Date Series properties sheet appears.

```
┌──────────────────────────────────────────────────┐
│  Date Series                                       │
│                                                    │
│  Series Name:     │FEDERAL SPENDING             │  │
│  Category Name:   │Year                         │  │
│  Value Name:      │Billions of Dollars          │  │
│                                                    │
│  First Category:  │1940                         │  │
│  Increment Each Category By                        │
│  ┌──────────┐                                      │
│  │5         │  ◉ Years ○ Months ○ Days ○ Weekdays  │
│  └──────────┘                                      │
│                        ┌──────┐   ┌─────────┐      │
│                        │ OK   │   │ Cancel  │      │
│                        └──────┘   └─────────┘      │
└──────────────────────────────────────────────────┘
```

You can move between the fields on the properties sheet by pressing the Tab key. As you do so, each of Chart's preset entries is highlighted and is replaced by anything you type. Type in the information shown on this sheet, and click OK. The properties sheet disappears and you can see that the titles you entered have been transferred to a series window.

Entering data

You are now ready to enter some data points. Simply type the numbers listed in the right column of this series window, pressing Enter after each to move to the next line. Since this is a Date series, Chart supplies all the dates. If you want to see all your entries at once, use the housekeeping skills you learned in Chapter 2 to move the series window up on the screen, and then drag its size box down to make it larger.

When the numbers are properly entered, click Plot Series and the chart window is transformed. If the chart window is obscured, click anyplace in it to bring it to the surface.

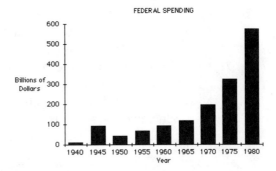

As you can see, this chart indicates that there has been quite a change in the spending habits of those who have controlled the nation's purse strings over the years. Let's enter another series and see how the fund raisers (those friendly folks at the IRS) are doing.

Tear another properties sheet from your unlimited supply by clicking first in the New Series window (you can see its edge behind the right side of the chart window) and again choosing Date from the Data menu.

Date Series

Series Name:	FEDERAL INCOME
Category Name:	Year
Value Name:	Billions of Dollars
First Category:	1940

Increment Each Category By

5	● Years ○ Months ○ Days ○ Weekdays

OK   Cancel

Except for the series name, which is the current time, Chart has already entered the same information on this properties sheet that you entered on the first one. Change the series name to Federal Income and click OK.

Note: When you want to plot more than one series on the same set of axes, it is important to keep the series type, first value, increment, and date unit identical. If you want to compare relationships where these parameters are different, plot

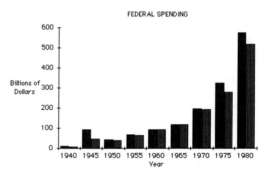

each series on a separate chart and then overlay one on the other—a process I will explain in another example.

Enter these numbers into the Federal Income series window, in the same manner that you filled in the Federal Spending window.

When the numbers are properly entered, click Plot Series and your chart is redrawn with both series plotted (click anyplace in the chart window to bring it to the surface).

Our chart shows a widening gap between what is coming in and what is going out, a condition known as deficit spending. Before moving on to other things, let's take a moment to spiff up this chart.

Cleaning up

The program uses the title of the first series plotted as the title for the chart. When there is more than one series, this title is usually no longer appropriate and must be edited. To edit the title, first select it by pointing at it and clicking the mouse button. The selected text is surrounded by black squares and the pointer, while it is over the text, assumes a new shape.

You can replace as much of the text as you like by placing the pointer in front of the first letter to be replaced, pressing the mouse button, dragging the pointer past the last letter to be replaced, and releasing the button. The letters you type now replace the highlighted section.

Change the title to Federal Budget, and, while the title is still selected, choose Text from the Format menu and click both Bold and Medium, to give the title more emphasis. The title's frame adjusts to its size, but not always the way you want it to. If the frame expands downward, displaying the title on two lines, drag the bottom right handle up and to the right to adjust the display.

```
┌─────────────────────────────────────────────────────────────┐
│ Text                                                          │
│                                                               │
│ Font                    Font Size        Automatic   Show     │
│ ⦿ Geneva    ☐ Italic    ○ Small          ☐ Text      ☐ Key    │
│ ○ New York  ⊠ Bold      ⦿ Medium         ⊠ Size      ☐ Value  │
│ ○ Chicago               ○ Large                               │
│                                                               │
│ Attached To             Orientation      Horizontal  Vertical │
│ ○ Unattached            ⦿ Horizontal     Alignment   Alignment│
│ ⦿ Chart Title           ○ Vertical       ○ Left      ○ Top    │
│ ○ Category Axis                          ⦿ Center    ⦿ Center │
│ ○ Value Axis                             ○ Right     ○ Bottom │
│ ○ Series or Data Point                                        │
│                                                               │
│ Series Number: [          ]                                   │
│ Point Number:  [          ]        ( OK )    ( Cancel )       │
└─────────────────────────────────────────────────────────────┘
```

If you had no further changes to make to the chart, you could click in the gray area outside the window to remove the squares marking the selected text. But we have more work to do, so after typing these corrections, move the selection squares by clicking the next thing that needs changing.

The next piece of text to work on is the value axis label, Billions of Dollars. This text takes up a lot of room beside the chart, and would probably convey the same information if it were a subtitle rather than a value label. Since this text is attached to the value axis, you can't simply move it. To convert the axis label to a subtitle, follow these steps:

■ Select the axis label by clicking it.

■ Drag through the text to highlight it.

■ Choose Cut from the Edit menu; the text disappears.

■ Click any blank space on the chart and choose Paste from the Edit menu; the text reappears.

■ Choose Text from the Format menu.

■ Click Chart Title under Attached To, and Medium under Font Size.

■ Adjust the size of the subtitle frame (if necessary) the same way you adjusted the title frame.

You now have both the main title and the subtitle attached as chart titles; when you click OK, the chart is redrawn with the new subtitle, surrounded by black squares, directly on top of the title. Move Billions of Dollars down by placing the pointer between any two of the black squares surrounding it and dragging downward.

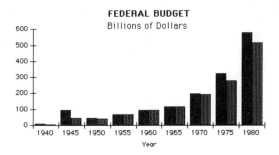

Adding a legend

A legend, showing which column represents income and which spending, can be added by choosing Add Legend from the Chart menu.

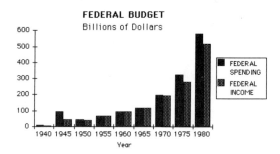

You can change the legend's position and layout by first selecting it (point and click) and then choosing Legend from the Format menu. The dialog box that appears gives you a variety of options. I left my legend in the default position, but you can experiment by clicking another option and then clicking OK. As with your other chart modifications, anything you do here can be reversed by returning to this dialog box and clicking the previous setting.

Adding a frame

As a final touch, you can frame your creation to set it off from any surrounding text. Framing is done in two quick and easy steps. The first step is selecting the entire chart by choosing Select Chart from the Chart menu. This causes the chart to be surrounded by the black selection squares.

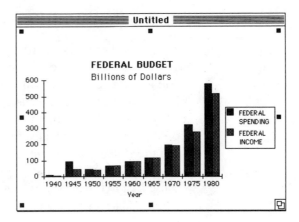

The second step is choosing Patterns from the Format menu and choosing the border pattern, weight, and style you want by clicking them.

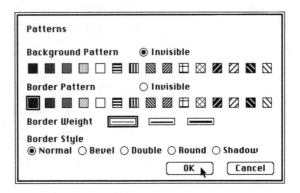

Your chart is redrawn surrounded by its new frame.

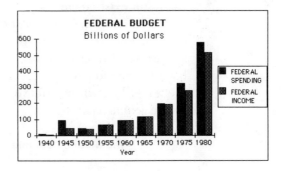

While the chart is still selected, you can return as many times as you like to the Patterns dialog box and click different combinations of pattern, weight, and style. You can even try a background pattern if you like, though they are often somewhat distracting.

Finishing a project

There are several ways to clear the desktop when you have finished one piece of work and want to start another. If there is a possibility you will want some portion of a presently plotted series on your new chart, you can store the series out of the way by unplotting them and closing the windows. This can be done either individually from the desktop, or collectively from the dialog box presented when you choose List from the Data menu. You can chart something else, and then again choose List to bring a series back to scavenge numbers.

However, since the format of your last chart will probably be changed when you start modifying your new chart, it is a good idea to save anything you may want to use again. Saving stores a copy of the information on the disk, and leaves the original in the program to continue working with.

You can save this chart by choosing Save As from the File menu and typing a name into the highlighted box.

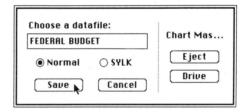

Click Save and pause for a moment while the chart and its format are stored safely on your disk. As you can see from your screen, saving a chart has no effect on the desktop—the chart still exists there. If you aren't going to use any of this chart's information on the next chart (you aren't), choose New from the File menu twice—once with a series window selected and a second time with the chart window selected—to clear both data and format.

We will now move on to create a variation of this simple column chart format.

The Stacked Column Chart

The stacked column chart displays several series by stacking them on top of one another.

For this example I will move to the next page in the *Statistical Abstract* and break our federal income down into four segments, according to its source. The chart we are going to create will cover, in five-year increments, the years between 1960 and 1980. It should end up looking like this.

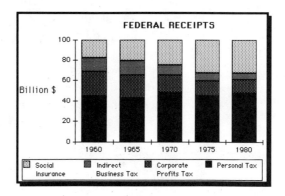

Creating the series

There are four series on this chart, each identical except for the name and numbers entered. I will lead you through the first series and then leave you on your own to duplicate the process for the rest.

Bring up a new properties sheet (first click in the New Series window if it is not already selected and then choose Date from the Data menu) and fill it in as I have filled in this one. Since the category labels (the years 1960 to 1980) adequately identify the category axis, a category name is not required. Press the Backspace key while the Category Name entry is highlighted to delete it.

Date Series

Series Name:	Personal Tax
Category Name:	
Value Name:	Billion $
First Category:	1960

Increment Each Category By

5   ● Years ○ Months ○ Days ○ Weekdays

[OK]   [Cancel]

Personal Tax	
Order: ▓▓▓▓	
☐ Plot Series	
	Billion $
1960	42.5
1965	51.4
1970	93.6
1975	127.5
1980	249.7

Entering data

Click OK on the properties sheet and then enter these numbers in your Personal Tax series window.

Fill out three more properties sheets and enter three more sets of numbers. You will notice that, with the exception of the series name, which you would have to change anyway, the Chart program automatically assigns the properties of the first series you create to each additional series. The only difference in each properties sheet is the series name: Corporate Profits Tax, Indirect Business Tax, Social Insurance.

Corporate Profits			Indirect Business T			Social Insurance		
Order: ▓▓▓▓			Order: ▓▓▓▓			Order: ▓▓▓▓		
☐ Plot Series			☐ Plot Series			☐ Plot Series		
	Billion $			Billion $			Billion $	
1960	22.3		1960	13.2		1960	16.7	
1965	27.1		1965	16.9		1965	24.5	
1970	33		1970	19.2		1970	49.2	
1975	41.8		1975	22.2		1975	91.9	
1980	70.6		1980	35.7		1980	171.3	

Enter the numbers in each series window just as they appear here. Click Plot Series in each series window as you finish filling it in, and watch the chart evolve.

When you have entered the data points for all four series and plotted them, you should have a chart that resembles this grouped column chart.

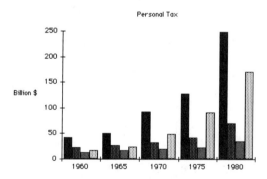

Changing the format from the menu

The easy way to convert a grouped column chart to a stacked column chart is by picking an icon from the Column Chart Gallery. If you choose Column from the Gallery menu, you are presented with this array of column chart options.

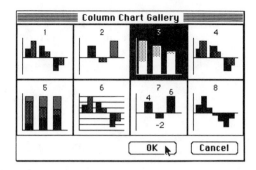

Clicking icon number 3 causes it to become highlighted. Click OK. The Column Chart Gallery disappears and your chart is redrawn as a stacked column chart.

Choosing from the gallery is the easy way to convert between formats, and probably the method you will normally use. The other method, which gives you more control over the chart's individual parameters, is not much more difficult. Before we set these parameters by hand, if you would like to try plotting your data points in a few other formats, pick a picture or two to emulate from the Column Chart Gallery. End up back with the simple column format, which is selection number 1 in the Column Chart Gallery.

Changing the format from the properties sheet

When you choose a chart format from a gallery, its parameters are recorded on a chart properties sheet similar in concept to the series properties sheets you have been filling out. To exercise more control over the individual parameters of the chart, you can call up that properties sheet by choosing Main Chart from the Format menu.

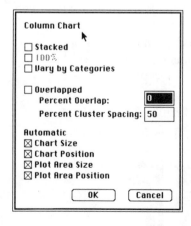

The controllable properties listed on these sheets vary slightly depending on the type of chart you are working with (bar, column, line, and so on). This is the chart properties sheet for a column chart. Study the choices carefully.

If you just make the obvious choice of Stacked, your grouped column chart is redrawn in this step format.

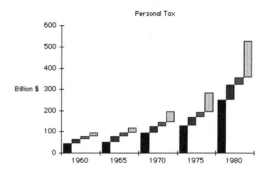

Since we don't want a step chart, click both Stacked and Overlapped, and then type 100 in the Percent Overlap box. When you click OK, your chart is redrawn to look like this.

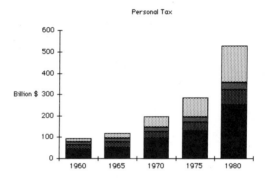

Although our five columns vary substantially in size, with the tallest having over five times the value of the shortest, each is made up of four components. To compare the change in the relative sizes of these four components, return to the Main Chart properties sheet and click 100%. (Of course, you could also select the 100-percent stacked column format from the Column Chart Gallery, but we're doing this the hard way.)

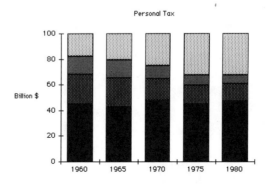

Your new chart makes it more obvious whose share of the burden has increased most over the years—at least it would if it had a legend to tell us who's who.

Adding a legend

The chart has four shaded segments, and you have no way of telling what each segment represents. There is an easy solution to this problem—just choose Add Legend from the Chart menu. Your chart is redrawn, making room for the legend that now appears along the right side.

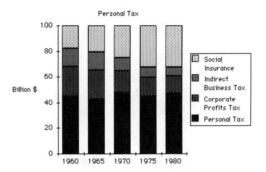

If you want to modify the legend, first select it by pointing and clicking anywhere on it. You can then choose Legend from the Format menu to display this dialog box.

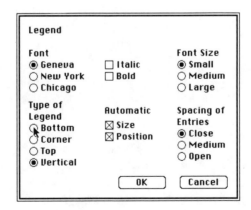

I have tried all the variations, and the only change I recommend is setting the Type of Legend to Bottom, allowing the chart to spread out a little.

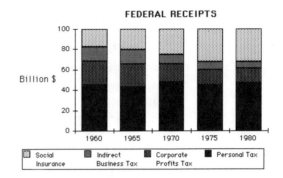

You may try other variations if you like; simply click your choice and then click OK. The chart is redrawn each time, but the legend stays selected, allowing you to jump right back to the Legend properties sheet to try other variations. If you decide not to make a change, you can click Cancel and return to the chart with no change.

Cleaning up

Next, you need to change the title, which is currently the title of the first series plotted (Personal Tax). Select it by pointing, clicking, and dragging, and then type the new title, Federal Receipts. While your new title is still selected, choose Text from the Format menu and click both Medium and Bold, to give the title more visual impact.

The chart title can be dragged up or down; as long as the program considers this text to be the main title, it restricts its movement to the vertical centerline of the chart. If you want to drag the title to either side, you first have to cut it and paste it back onto the chart, which makes it unattached. For now, let's leave it where it is. The black handles around the title go away when you make another selection.

While you are modifying text, select the value axis label, Billion $, and again choose Text from the Format menu, this time clicking only Medium.

Adding a frame

Your chart is now pretty as a picture; all it needs is a frame. To add a frame, you first select the entire chart (choose

Select Chart from the Chart menu) to designate what the frame will be applied to.

Next choose Patterns from the Format menu, and pick a pattern for the border—I think basic black is best. Note that there are both background pattern selections and border pattern selections. If you accidentally click the black background selection, your chart will be covered with a solid black rectangle; don't panic, you can return to the Patterns properties sheet and correct the mistake.

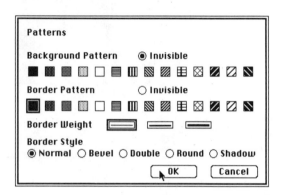

Your chart is redrawn with what is called the Normal frame. You can do quite a bit of experimentation at this point. By returning to the Patterns dialog box, you can vary the border pattern, weight, and style—even the background pattern. Try a few variations if you like. The example at the beginning of this section was done with an invisible background, a black border in medium weight, and a shadow frame.

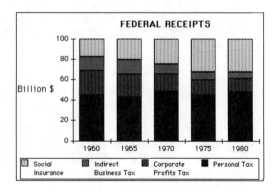

When you are through framing your masterpiece, save it by choosing Save As from the File menu, or don't save it and simply send it off to oblivion by clearing both format and data (choose New from the File menu with the chart window selected, and again with a series window selected).

The Deviation Column Chart

Chart automatically creates a net deviation column chart, such as this one, if you enter both positive and negative numbers in the series window.

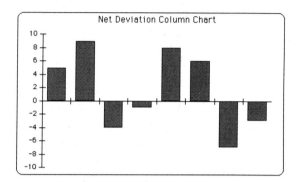

All that is required for a deviation column chart is a mixture of positive and negative numbers. This format is typically used to show business profits and losses, but not everything below the base line is a loss, and you often see this format used to express corporate profits that are indexed on a median year or that are shown as a change from a previous year.

CORPORATE PROFITS
(in billions of dollars)

Year	1960	1965	1970	1975	1980
After-tax Profits	29.1	46.3	41.3	81.4	157.8

This table lists the cumulative after-tax profits of all U.S. Corporations at five-year intervals from 1960 to 1980, in billions of dollars. We are going to express this information in a few different forms.

Create a Date series with a series name of Corporate Profits, a category name that is blank (type a Backspace to remove the X supplied by the program), a value name of Billions, a first category of 1960, and an increment of 5 Years. Enter the values shown in the table, and plot the series. You should end up with a simple column chart looking like this.

You can quickly create another series showing the difference in corporate profits between successive time increments. First click the Plot Series box in the original series window to remove it from the chart and then choose Analyze from the Data menu. Clicking Difference in the resulting dialog box creates another series window, titled Difference of Corporate Profits. Clicking the Plot Series box in the Difference series window produces this chart.

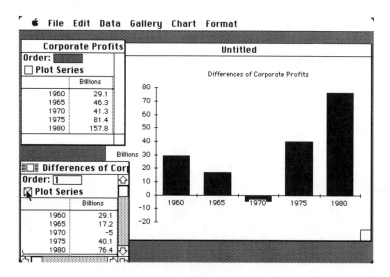

The Range Column Chart

The range column format requires some manipulation on your part. It is a stocky version of the automatically generated high-low chart (available from the Line Chart Gallery), and is only worth the extra effort if you particularly prefer it.

The finished chart for this example should look like this one, which displays the normal monthly temperature range in Seattle, based on a 30-year average. The table beside the chart contains the information used in its creation.

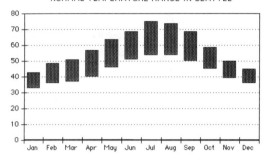

NORMAL TEMPERATURE RANGE IN SEATTLE

Month	Minimum	Maximum	Difference
Jan	33	43	10
Feb	36	49	13
Mar	37	51	14
Apr	40	57	17
May	46	64	18
Jun	51	69	18
Jul	54	75	21
Aug	54	74	20
Sep	50	69	19
Oct	45	59	14
Nov	39	50	11
Dec	36	45	9

To create this chart, fill out two Date Series properties sheets, one like this and a second one identical except for the series name, which is Difference. The series names will not appear on the finished chart. They are only used to keep track of the series windows while you are working on them.

Date Series

Series Name:	Minimum
Category Name:	
Value Name:	

| First Category: | Jan |

Increment Each Category By

| 1 | ○ Years ● Months ○ Days ○ Weekdays |

[OK]   [Cancel]

Enter the data points into the series windows: The values are taken from the Minimum and Difference columns of the table. The values in the Difference column reflect the *difference* between the high end of the range and the low end. The reason for using the difference rather than the high and low points will be obvious when we modify the chart. To cause only the month to be displayed in the categories column, choose Categories from the Format menu and click off everything except Months under Show.

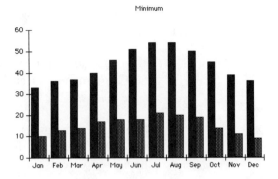

The initial plotting of these two series is a simple column chart. Change the format to a stacked column chart by selecting number 3 from the Column Chart Gallery.

Now select the bottom segments of the columns by placing the pointer over any bottom segment and clicking; your selection is indicated by the appearance of a small white circle in three of the bottom segments.

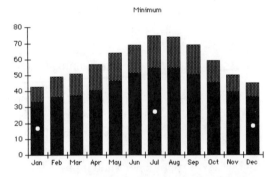

Choose Patterns from the Format menu and click Invisible for both Area Patterns and Border Patterns. Your chart is redrawn to look like this. The bottom segments of the columns are still there; they have just been shaded with the same pattern as their background.

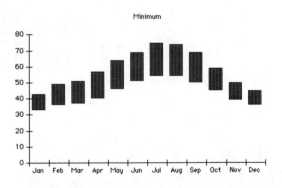

This chart is almost what you started out to create. Here are the steps required to finish the chart:

■ To add the grid in the background, choose Axes from the Chart menu and click Major Grid Lines under For Values Show.

■ To lighten the grid lines, select one of them and then choose Patterns from the Format menu and click one of the lighter patterns (like the fourth one from the left).

■ To frame the plot area, choose Select Plot Area from the Chart menu and, again, choose Patterns from the Format menu, this time clicking the solid black border pattern.

■ To add the proper title, select and edit Minimum, and set the size and weight on the properties sheet presented when you choose Text from the Format menu.

If you follow these steps, your chart is rapidly converted to the one you set out to produce.

The Floating Column Chart

The floating column chart, called a gross deviation column chart by some, is distinguished by the fact that its columns have two segments that "float" on either side of the zero base line. We will use this format to see how a hypothetical company's net annual profit has varied over the years, as compared with its gross income. This illustration shows the finished chart and the table of values used to create it.

YEAR	GROSS INCOME		EXPENSES	NET INCOME
1970	97	T	90	7
1971	114	H	106	8
1972	122	O	110	12
1973	128	U	113	15
1974	135	S	115	20
1975	138	A	120	18
1976	147	N	122	25
1977	147	D	120	27
1978	160		125	35
1979	172	$	130	42

Distribution of Gross Income

As with the range column chart, a little manipulation of the data is required before plotting. Each column on this chart represents the values associated with one year in two different series; an Expenses series, and a Net Income series. The sum of these two series for any year is the year's gross income.

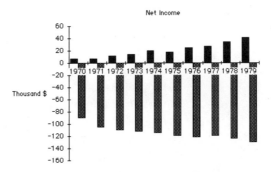

Date Series

Series Name:	Net Income
Category Name:	
Value Name:	Thousand $
First Category:	1970

Increment Each Category By

| 1 | ⦿ Years ○ Months ○ Days ○ Weekdays |

OK   Cancel

To create this chart, first fill out two Date Series properties sheets, one like this and the other with the name Expenses. Fill in both series windows, using the values in the Net Income column of the table for the Net Income series window, and the *negative* of the values in the Expenses column for the Expenses series; for example, for the 1970 expenses, enter −90 instead of 90. When you click the Plot Series boxes in both windows, this chart is produced.

It's still a ways from the finished product, isn't it? I will list several intermediate steps that you can go through on your own, and then will pick you up for the finishing touches.

■ Select the value-axis label (Thousand $).

■ Choose Text from the Format menu and click Vertical under Orientation and Medium under Font Size.

■ Choose Main Chart from the Format menu; click Over-lapped and fill in 100 as the Percent Overlap.

■ Select the category (horizontal) axis.

■ Choose Axis from the Format menu and click Low under Tick Label Position.

Your chart should now resemble this one.

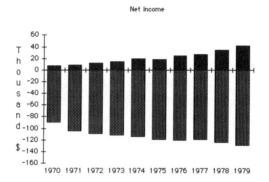

To finish the chart off, change the title to Distribu-tion of Gross Income, insert the label Net Income on the upper part of the chart, and Expenses on the lower part, and frame the plot area. You are now left with only one task—disposing of the minus signs in front of the numbers below 0 on the vertical axis. This can be done very easily in Chart, by dragging an insertion box over the unwanted symbols, typing a Space (to allow you to choose Patterns from the Format menu), and assigning a white background and border pattern to the box. The box now blends in with the background, thereby hiding the minus signs.

Another method is to transfer the chart to the Mac-Paint program and simply erase the unwanted symbols. Either way, you should end up with a chart that looks like this one.

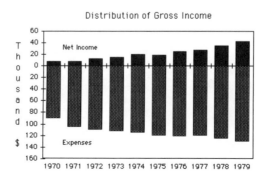

In the process of creating these column charts, you have used many of the Chart program's features. As you apply the skills you have developed in this chapter to other chart formats in the remainder of the book, you will practice using these features and be introduced to new ones.

The
Bar
Chart

As you work your way through this chapter, you'll see examples of the standards that apply specifically to bar charts—both simple varieties and those that are not-so-simple. In the second half of the chapter, you will apply these standards while creating bar charts of both varieties, with the assistance of Microsoft's Chart program and the Macintosh.

Standards

Bar charts are, in essence, column charts rotated 90 degrees to the right. The bar chart is just as simple and easy to understand as the column chart, and is possibly a little more popular—at least it gets more credit since many people refer to both formats as bar charts.

The bar chart is an alternative to the column chart initially created when you enter information into a series window and click the Plot Series box. As with column charts, you can browse through a gallery of prototypical formats, choose one, and then tailor it to your specific needs.

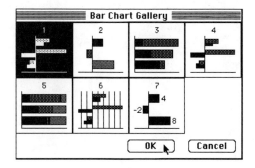

The Simple Bar Chart

The most obvious difference between column and bar charts is the orientation of the base line. On a simple bar chart, this line is the vertical axis, usually on the left side of the page. The bars originate at this base and extend to the right, their length indicating an amount or percentage.

A more subtle difference between column and bar charts lies in the way they are used. The bar chart usually compares different items at a specific point in time, whereas the column chart shows variations in one item over a period of time.

Most of the rules of composition and methods of construction that are true for the column chart also apply to the bar chart. I will review them, for those who came in late.

Placement of bars

A bar chart can have as few as one bar or as many as you can fit on the page; fifty bars (representing the states, for example) are not at all uncommon.

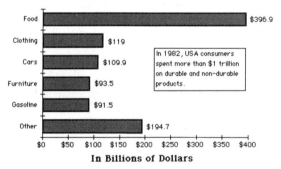

What We Buy

In Billions of Dollars

You can specify, in the Chart program, the spacing you would like between the plotted bars: You may space them evenly, push them together, or arrange them in groups. If the bars are to be evenly spaced, each should be separated from its neighbor by a space about equal to half the width of one bar.

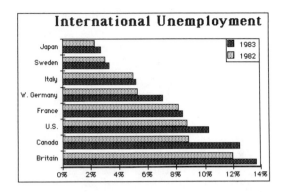

When more than one series is plotted you can arrange the bars in groups, with each group containing a bar for each series. When you group the bars in this manner, a space proportionate to the number of bars in the group should be left between each cluster of bars.

When working with a grouped bar chart, you can specify whether you would like the individual bars in a group to be slightly apart, touching, or overlapping. If you are using a substantial overlap, try to arrange the different series in order of diminishing value to avoid overlapping short bars with long ones, which makes them appear skinny and less important. When using Chart, experimenting with decisions such as these and seeing their effect is a matter of a few clicks of the mouse.

Shading and patterns

Bars can be shaded or hatched to add interest, to emphasize a point, or to differentiate between the boys, girls, and . . . whatever.

Be consistent about the order of shades and patterns—generally start with the darkest at the bottom and work up. The Chart program automatically distributes the patterns in the order they appear on the Patterns properties sheet. This distribution can be depended on to look good through the first five shades; after that the patterns may clash when placed side-by-side. Here is a display of all the patterns offered by the program—the adjacent diagonally patterned bars demonstrate why it is important to pick your patterns carefully.

This advice is given from a design point of view, but a nice design may not be your main objective. If you are trying to prove a point or influence a decision, remember that the darkest bar gets the most attention. It appears larger, closer, and more important than a lighter bar of the same size. So if the bar you want to emphasize can't be placed on the bottom, you might try a different approach when plotting your information. At your request, Chart computes and plots the growth, trend, or average value of your series. Other approaches that may give a different perspective on the same information are plotting the percentage of change within a series, or indexing all values in the series to an arbitrary value and plotting the resulting relationship.

Don't be concerned if you find concepts like trend, percentage of change, and indexing confusing right now—I will show you how to use each of these techniques as you create charts of various types.

The people who look at your graph form their first impressions based on its neatness, lack of clutter, and the patterns you select for shading and emphasis. Pick the plumage for your plottings as carefully as you do your wardrobe—unless your idea of proper attire for all occasions is jeans and a T-shirt.

Order

If your chart has an abundance of bars, you have one more decision to make: What order should you put them in? This decision is influenced strongly by the purpose of the chart (a decision you should already have made). The most common methods of arranging bars are alphabetic order, numeric order, or a combination of the two.

An alphabetic listing allows the reader to locate a specific category more readily, but the ragged right edge makes comparisons difficult.

A numeric listing makes the rank or relative position of each bar obvious, but you may have trouble finding a specific bar. For the best of both worlds, the two possibilities can be placed side-by-side.

Sorting the items in your series into some order— ascending or descending, alphabetic or numeric—is another one of those little housekeeping chores a computer can do for you, either in a spreadsheet program or in the Chart program itself. (I'll get into the mechanics of this task later.)

An occasional alternative to ordering your bars alphabetically or numerically is to arrange them in chronological order. This method is appropriate for a bar chart that displays a few selected dates or periods of time, but a trend that involves equal time intervals over a long period is better displayed on a column or line chart.

The simple bar chart is a versatile format for presenting a numeric relationship to your audience, but it isn't the only variety of bar chart available. Some of the following formats are created automatically, by simply selecting the appropriate icon from the Bar Chart Gallery; others require your intervention and direction. In the next sections, I will discuss several of the more exotic bar chart formats, then we will fire up the Macintosh and produce them. Using Chart to create these formats might require the innovative application of several commands, but once you have mastered the method you can create them in minutes.

The Subdivided Bar Chart

The bar chart that is analogous to the previous chapter's stacked column chart is the subdivided bar chart. The name has been changed to better relate to the horizontal orientation of the bar, but the standards that apply to its creation are the same. In the following chart variation, which is an alternative to the grouped bar chart for showing the relationship between two or more series, the individual bars from each series are laid end to end, to form a subdivided bar.

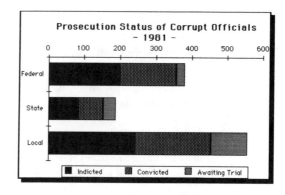

The subdivided bar segments can be identified in the same manner as the stacked column segments, with each division corresponding to an amount or a percentage of the whole. If the bar stretches the entire width of the chart, you have a 100-percent subdivided bar chart.

If you only have a few subdivided bars on your chart, they can be displayed dramatically by using this step format. Converting to this format from the straight subdivided bar chart is just a matter of clicking a different option with the mouse.

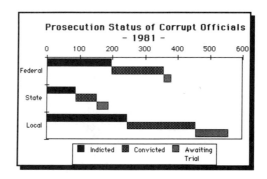

Shading and patterns

When different shades and patterns are used in segments of the same bar, they should be used in order, from darkest to lightest, with the darkest nearest the beginning of the bar—the side of the bar that is against the vertical axis.

The Paired Bar Chart

The paired bar chart allows you to compare two sets of values that apply to the same list of category items.

You can list the category labels either down the center of the chart or along one side; either way, on a paired bar chart the zero line drops down the center and bars extend to the right and left. Since each side has its own horizontal value axis, and therefore its own scale, it is possible to compare quantities expressed in different units or magnitudes. The values most significant to you should extend to the right of the zero line and should have a darker shade or pattern.

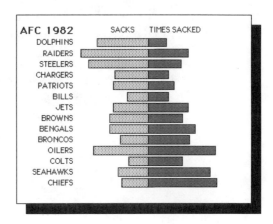

The Deviation Bar Chart

The deviation bar chart allows you to show positive and negative change, in either percentages or absolute numbers. You show this change by plotting positive values to the right of a center line that represents zero and negative values to the left. When creating a deviation bar chart, if logic allows, you should arrange the positive values in descending order and the negative in ascending order.

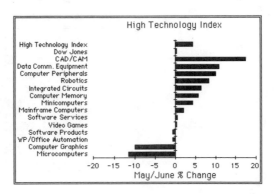

The Range Bar Chart

When the values of several items consistently vary between a high and a low, as with the temperature in different cities over a period of time or the pay scale for a trade in various regions of the nation, a range bar chart can be used to make an effective comparison.

RANGE OF MONTHLY ELECTRIC BILL

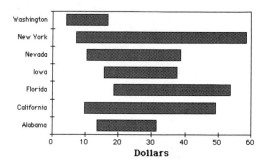

Each bar starts at the minimum value of the item associated with it and extends to the maximum value. Sometimes the bar is marked at the point representing the average value.

The Sliding Bar Chart

The sliding bar chart consists of one or more bars, each representing all there is of a particular item. Each bar "slides" across a center line, with the portion extending on either side indicating that side's share of the item.

COMPOSITION OF SELECTED STATE LOWER HOUSES

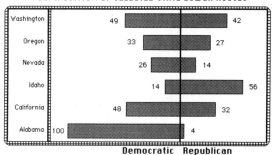

On this sliding bar chart, the total length of each bar represents the number of members in a specific state's House of Representatives. The segment to the left is the number of Democrats; the segment to the right is the number of Republicans.

Judging from this chart, Alabama is not the place to seek your fortune in politics if you are a Republican.

Both sides of the bar can be further subdivided. These divisions were made arbitrarily, for the purpose of demonstration, but the principle could be used to divide each group into male and female representatives, honest and dishonest politicians, or any other dichotomy.

COMPOSITION OF SELECTED STATE LOWER HOUSES

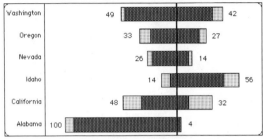

Democratic Republican

A specialized variation of the sliding bar chart, the population pyramid, deals with the distribution of two classifications of people (such as male-female or black-white) within defined categories (such as age).

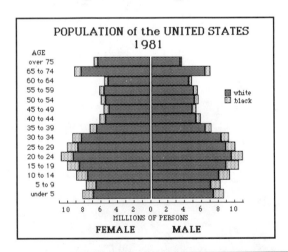

Creating Bar Charts

As you can see from the above examples, the major difference in appearance between bar charts and column charts is the orientation of the bars (columns). Using the Chart program, you can create a simple bar chart and the variations on it in much the same manner you created column charts in Chapter 5.

The only difference is that at some point you have to choose a bar chart format (either from the Bar Chart Gallery or with the Chart Type command from the Chart menu). You can make this choice at any time—even after Chart has presented your information in the preselected column format.

Now let's create a few of the variations we looked at in the first part of this chapter.

The Simple Bar Chart

For our first example, let's create this simple bar chart, which compares the percentage of nonproduction workers employed in several industries during 1947 and 1982. Nonproduction workers range from mailroom clerks to chairmen of the board—anybody who doesn't directly contribute to producing the product that brings in the profit.

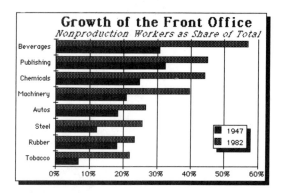

This chart is composed of two series each displaying the values of nine items at one point in time—an application which precisely matches the defined purpose of a bar chart.

To pick the format in which you would like Chart to plot your data points, browse through the Bar Chart Gallery (position the pointer over the Gallery menu title, press the mouse button, drag the pointer to Bar, release the button), and select the miniature chart that most closely resembles the desired result. Number 1 would be a good selection for this chart. After you have clicked the appropriate chart and confirmed your choice by clicking OK, the Gallery goes away and you can create your chart, confident that it will appear in the selected format.

Creating a series

As always, you should start with a clean desktop; if you have been working on other charts, save anything you would like to use again and clear the work area (choose New from the File menu with the chart window selected, and again with a series window selected).

The category labels on this chart are words that you have to type in; you therefore want to define the series as a text series. Do this by choosing Text from the Data menu and filling in the Text Series properties sheet.

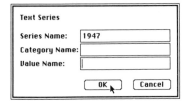

The information stored on the properties sheet becomes part of the series and is saved, retrieved and copied along with the series. You want only the series name (1947) on this properties sheet—the category and value axes are self explanatory and therefore need no names. Select each unused name and enter a backspace to remove the entry supplied by Chart. Remember that you can move the highlight indicating the field you are editing by pressing the Tab key, and that text insertion, deletion, and other normal editing techniques can be applied. When your Text Series properties sheet looks like mine, click OK to return to the desktop.

Entering data

You now have a properly titled series window into which you can enter some data points.

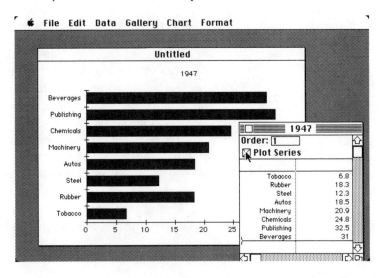

Type the first category label, press Enter, type its value, and press Enter again. Repeat this process for the other points, until your series window looks like this (I enlarged the window and moved it for this display). Click Plot Series and you are presented with the simple bar chart you see plotted behind the series window.

Entering the second series

The properties sheet and series window for the second series are almost identical to those for the first, so let's use a shortcut to save a little typing while creating the series.

■ Select the entire first series by clicking anyplace in the empty band above the columns, where the category and value names would appear if you had not deleted them. All lines become highlighted.

■ Choose Copy from the Edit menu. A copy of the series is stored on the clipboard.

■ Select the New Series window and choose Paste from the Edit menu. A new series is created and the data you copied from the 1947 series window is pasted into it.

■ Choose Text from the Data menu and change the second series name from the time to 1982.

■ Click OK to return to the desktop.

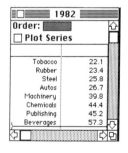

Since you don't intend to plot two identical series, you must make a few changes to the copy. You could replace each number in the value column by selecting it (double-click) and typing the new one, shown here; but you can save a lot of clicking by selecting the top number, typing its replacement, and pressing the Enter key twice to move the selection highlight past the categories entry and on to the next value entry.

If you plot your new series (click Plot Series in its window), it joins the first series on your chart, which then resembles the one shown here. I think you will agree that cutting and pasting is far easier than entering a new series from scratch.

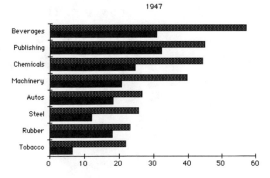

Modifying the chart

You have created a chart that is very similar to the one you set out to duplicate; it is now time to add the finishing touches: a new title, a legend, and a frame.

The title that Chart automatically supplied for your creation is the title of the series you chose to plot first, in this case 1947. This title is fine if there is only one series, but is not usually appropriate otherwise. Growth of the Front Office would be a better title for this chart. Don't be tempted to go back to the properties sheet and change the title—that's where the legend gets its identifying information, and 1947 is still appropriate for that.

Changing the chart's title is as simple as selecting it (point and click), dragging through it, and typing the new one. It will probably take you less time to do it than to read about doing it. Since the new title is quite a bit longer than the old one, it may appear on two lines. If so, you can display it on one line by dragging a corner handle to lengthen the title's insertion box.

While you have the title selected, make it larger and bolder and have the Macintosh display it in a different font. You can do all this on the Text properties sheet that comes up when you choose Text from the Format menu. I used the New York font in the Large size, and clicked Bold for my title.

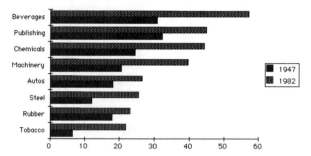

Adding the legend is an easy modification; all you have to do is ask for it by choosing Add Legend from the Chart menu. Your chart should now resemble this one. You can move the legend by selecting it and dragging it with the mouse, or you can change its format by choosing Legend from the Format menu and opting for a top, bottom, or corner display.

You can balance the top-heaviness of this chart by tucking the legend into the lower right corner. Drag it down, so that it is opposite the bar labeled Rubber and above the number 50 on the horizontal axis.

You can now add a set of major grid lines to the value axis (choose Axes from the Chart menu and click Major Grid Lines under Values). Then select the legend, choose Patterns from the Format menu, and change the border style to Shadow, for a little more dramatic effect. When you click OK, your chart is redrawn to look like this one.

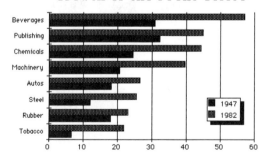

Here are the steps I followed to add the finishing touches to this chart:

■ Add the percent symbol to the values on the horizontal axis by first selecting the 1947 series window and then choosing Values from the Format menu and typing the symbol (%) in the Text After box; the symbol is automatically appended to all value axis labels on the chart.

■ Add the subtitle *Nonproduction Workers as Share of Total* just below the main title. While the subtitle is still selected, choose Text from the Format menu and click New York, Italic, and Medium.

■ Frame the chart by selecting it (choose Select Chart from the Chart menu), choosing Patterns from the Format menu, and picking your border pattern, weight, and style. Since you have already used the Shadow frame on the legend, you should stick with it here.

That's all there is to the first example. Your chart should now look like the one we started out to reproduce; you can now save it or print it.

The Subdivided Bar Chart

For our next example, let's take a look at several of the highest-paying positions in the nation. In May, 1983, the magazine *U.S. News and World Report* published the results of a poll, in which they listed the salary and bonuses of the 916 top executives in the United States.

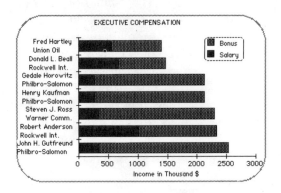

This subdivided bar chart shows how the total pay of seven of these executives is distributed between salary and bonuses. It appears from this chart that peddling pork bellies can bring home a lot of bacon.

Creating a series

This set of data points is another text type series, so choose Text from the Data menu and enter a series name (Salary) and category and value names (Name and Company, Income in Thousand $) on the properties sheet.

Entering data

The properties sheet goes away when you click OK, and a series window appears. You are going to enter some rather long labels in the category column; a few formatting changes will make the information more presentable. If you choose Categories from the Format menu and click Align Left, the text typed is aligned with the left edge of the category column. If you enlarge the series window and slide the column dividers to the right, as I have done for the next illustration, you can see your entire entry at one time.

Name and Company	Income in Thousand $
John H. Gutfreund//Philbro-Salomon	344.495
Robert Anderson//Rockwell Int.	997.083
Steven J. Ross//Warner Comm.	350
Henry Kaufman//Philbro-Salomon	264.495
Gedale Horowitz//Philbro-Salomon	264.495
Donald L. Beall//Rockwell Int.	668.333
Fred Hartley//Union Oil	561.667

Type each person's name and company into the left column, press Enter, type the salary (in thousands, with no dollar sign or comma) into the right column, press Enter again. The double-slash between the person's name and the company name causes the information to be printed on two lines when it appears on the chart as a tick-mark label. As you will see shortly, the slashes are not printed on the chart.

After you have entered all the information for the first series, use the the Copy and Paste commands from the Edit menu to duplicate the series. Change the series name and replace the salary figures in the duplicate series window with the bonuses shown here.

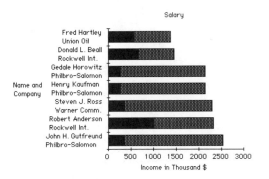

Choose a subdivided format (number 3) from the Bar Chart Gallery, and then choose the List command from the Data menu. Clicking the two Plot boxes and then the OK button causes a chart to be plotted with both series on it.

Modifying the chart

There are only a few changes required to clean this chart up. I don't think the category axis title, Name and Company, is really necessary. To eliminate this title, select it and then drag the pointer through it so all the text becomes highlighted. Now choose Clear from the Edit menu. The title disappears and, as soon as you click someplace else to remove the selection handles, the chart is redrawn to fill the space vacated by the title. Replace the chart title, Salary, by selecting it and typing the new title, Executive Compensation. The new title looks more impressive if you choose Text from the Format menu and change it to a large, bold typeface. Add a legend and a frame and you have a chart that matches what we set out to create.

The Deviation Bar Chart

A deviation bar chart shows values that extend one direction or the other from a base line of zero.

In addition to plotting changes in absolute values, such as profits and losses, a deviation bar chart can illustrate fluctuations in values that don't change sign (plus to minus or minus to plus) by plotting the percent of change. This is one such chart, which plots the percent of change in an index of selected high-technology stocks.

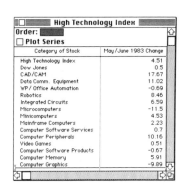

You can create this chart by selecting the simplest bar chart format from the gallery (number 2) and entering information; there are no exotic manipulations required. Fill out a Text Series properties sheet and a series window, using the information in this series window. As with the last chart, if you want to see all your information at one time you have to make adjustments to the series window and its two columns.

When discussing charting standards earlier in this chapter, I pointed out that with a deviation bar chart the segments should be arranged in descending order. Use Chart's Sort command to organize the information you have just entered.

Choose Sort from the Data menu. This dialog box appears, allowing you to rearrange the series by sorting the information based on either the category column or the value column of the selected series window.

Since the category column contains text, sorting it would simply arrange the entries in alphabetical order, leaving the values in an unorganized state and making the chart no easier to read. Sorting the value column, on the other hand, gives you precisely what you want. Click both By Value and In Ascending Order; when you click OK the series is rearranged. If it seems backwards to sort the series in ascending order, remember that the categories that are ordered from top to bottom in the series window go from bottom to top on the chart—the top item in the series window is plotted closest to the horizontal axis.

Notice on the chart you are trying to duplicate, that the High Technology and Dow Jones Indexes, which represent composites of broad classifications of stocks, are placed at the top of the list, rather than in their respective slots in the numeric order. The easiest way to move these entries to the top is to cut and paste them. Move one line at a time by first selecting it (drag across the line; it becomes highlighted) and then choosing Cut from the Edit menu. The line disappears from the list and is stored on the Clipboard. If you now point at the space just below the last item on the list and click the mouse button, the H-beam appears there and, if you choose Paste from the Edit menu, the line you just cut reappears at the bottom of the list (remember the plotting order). When everything is arranged correctly in your series window, select format number 2 from the Bar Chart Gallery and click Plot Series.

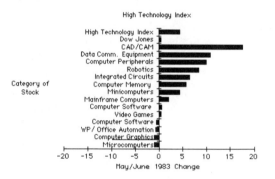

As you can see, the tick labels, which are automatically positioned next to the axis, obscure the negative bars. This is easily remedied by first selecting the vertical axis, then choosing Axis from the Format menu and clicking Low, under Tick Label Position. When the chart is redrawn, the tick labels are at the left edge of the plot area.

If you remove the category name, enlarge the title, and frame this chart, you have done what you set out to do.

Charts like the samples you have just created are easily produced using Chart's gallery of standard formats to set the basic style. There are a few other variations, however, that require a little manipulation to create. We will now work our way through several of these.

The Paired Bar Chart

You will find many subjects other than high finance illustrated with charts; for example, this paired bar chart uses data from the sports section of the *Seattle Times*.

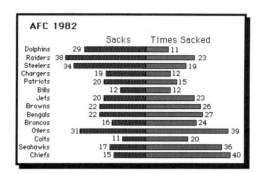

In this chart, the number of times in 1982 that each listed team's quarterback was sacked, is compared to the number of times the same team sacked the opponent's quarterback. (Sacking, for non-football fans, is what happens when all the guys on the team that doesn't have possession of the ball manage to pile on top of the other team's quarterback before he can throw the ball away.)

The format of this chart is not one that the Chart program automatically produces. It differs from standard formats primarily in that the value axis is positive in both directions from zero—that is, the number of Sacks is positive, and the number of Times Sacked is also positive. There are several ways to produce this chart, and the method you choose determines how you have to enter the numbers. I will lead you through the steps in producing this chart by one method, and then give you a general idea of another. As you practice using the Chart program you will discover many shortcuts and specialized techniques for producing intricate charts in unusual formats.

If you were paying attention as we produced our previous charts, you can probably look at this one and guess that it was created with two series: one listing the number of times each team's quarterback was sacked, and the other listing the number of times each team sacked the opposing quarterback. That is one method, but we will use another, involving three series, as shown on this chart.

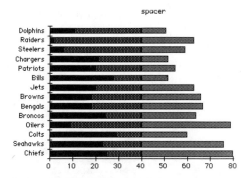

spacer

Our finished paired bar chart is really just a three-segment subdivided bar chart with the first segment and both axes removed. The first segment is simply a spacer, filling the space between the vertical axis and the beginning of the Sacks segment. Since the right end of all the Sacks segments have to line up, the spacer segments have to be of varying lengths. The length of the spacer is chosen to make the sum of the spacer and the Sacks segments always equal the same number. This number should be slightly more than the longest Sacks segment, which is 38. Forty would be a good number.

Create a spacer series (text type), listing the teams in the category column and a number in the value column equal to 40 minus the number of sacks by that team.

The finished series contains these numbers. Copy the series to the Clipboard (drag through the series to highlight all entries, and choose Copy from the Edit menu). Then select the New Series window and paste the copied series there. The disk drive hums for a while and another series window is formed and filled with the copied data points. When the humming stops, select the New Series window again and again choose Paste from the Edit menu. You now have a total of three series windows filled with the names of football teams.

Select the second window, choose Text from the Data menu, and rename the series Sacks. Select the third series and rename it Times Sacked. Edit the Sacks and Times Sacked series windows, replacing the numbers with those shown here.

To edit a list of numbers in a text series, double-click the top number to select it, type the new number, and then press the Enter key twice. The first time you press the Enter key the highlight jumps to the next category label; the second time it jumps to the next value entry.

spacer	
Order: ▓▓▓▓	
☐ Plot Series	
Chiefs	25
Seahawks	23
Colts	29
Oilers	9
Broncos	24
Bengals	18
Browns	18
Jets	20
Bills	28
Patriots	20
Chargers	21
Steelers	6
Raiders	2
Dolphins	11

Sacks		Times Sacked	
Order: ▓▓▓▓		Order: ▓▓▓▓	
☐ Plot Series		☐ Plot Series	
Chiefs	15	Chiefs	40
Seahawks	17	Seahawks	36
Colts	11	Colts	20
Oilers	31	Oilers	39
Broncos	16	Broncos	24
Bengals	22	Bengals	27
Browns	22	Browns	26
Jets	20	Jets	23
Bills	12	Bills	12
Patriots	20	Patriots	15
Chargers	19	Chargers	12
Steelers	34	Steelers	19
Raiders	38	Raiders	23
Dolphins	29	Dolphins	11

Select format number 3 from the Bar Chart Gallery, and then plot all three series, either by clicking their Plot Series boxes or by choosing List from the Data menu and clicking the Plot boxes there. This chart is produced.

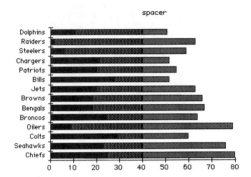

The scaling on the horizontal axis is inappropriate, and the first segment in each bar is not wanted, but you can see the finished chart starting to emerge. Here are the steps required to complete the chart.

■ Select one of the black segments, by clicking it, and then choose Patterns from the format menu. Click Invisible for both Area and Border Pattern to get rid of all the black segments.

■ Choose Axes from the Chart menu and eliminate both axes by clicking off all the boxes except the one for categories tick mark labels (the team names).

■ Replace the chart's present title, Spacer, with the word Sacks, followed by eight spaces, then Times Sacked. With eight spaces, the titles are placed about right when you enlarge them to the medium-size font by choosing Text from the Format menu and clicking Medium.

■ Insert the title AFC 1982 in the upper corner and then choose Text from the Format menu and change this new title by clicking Bold and Medium.

■ Frame your chart by choosing Select Chart from the Chart menu, then choosing Patterns from the Format menu and selecting a border pattern (I chose a solid black, heavyweight, shadow-style border).

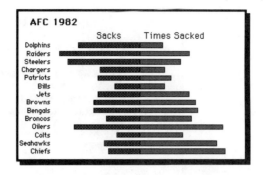

There is only one thing left to do to your chart: add some numbers or a scale. Either of these tasks can be done in the Chart program, but are much more easily done in MacPaint. More is said about the MacPaint program in Chapter 11, but here is a little hint to get you started. If you look at the Chart menu while the chart window is selected, you will see that Copy has changed to Copy Chart. Choosing Copy Chart copies the chart to the Clipboard, from whence it can be pasted to the Scrapbook or to MacPaint.

A second method of creating this chart is as a deviation bar chart (format number 1 from the gallery). Use two series—Sacks and Times Sacked—but multiply each value in the Sacks series by minus one (− 1). After the chart is plotted, choose Main Chart from the Format menu and specify a 100-percent overlap (but not stacked).

The Range Bar Chart

A range bar chart, as its name implies, displays fluctuation extremes by plotting a bar from an item's low value to its high value. You can use the same technique to create this chart that you used to create the range column chart in the last chapter: Plot two series and then (presto change-o and a puff of smoke) make one invisible. This technique is demonstrated by the next example.

We are going to plot the differences in the rate at which certain states tax the personal income of their inhabitants. The rate is usually dependent on the amount of income, and ranges from nothing at all to whatever the traffic will bear. For the sake of simplicity, our chart only displays the first ten states (selected alphabetically).

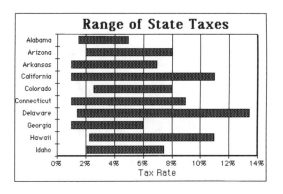

This chart is composed of two series. Fill out two Text Series properties sheets; name the first series Low and the second Range. The category name for both is State; the value name is Tax Rate. This table shows the low, high, and range of taxes (high − low) of each of these ten states.

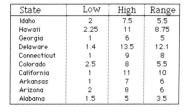

State	Low	High	Range
Idaho	2	7.5	5.5
Hawaii	2.25	11	8.75
Georgia	1	6	5
Delaware	1.4	13.5	12.1
Connecticut	1	9	8
Colorado	2.5	8	5.5
California	1	11	10
Arkansas	1	7	6
Arizona	2	8	6
Alabama	1.5	5	3.5

When you have entered the low and range values into the appropriate series windows (use Copy and Paste to move the state names to the second window), choose a subdivided (stacked) bar chart format (number 3) from the gallery and then return to the series windows and click both Plot Series boxes, making sure you click Low first, and then Range. Remember that the order in which you click the Plot Series boxes determines which series is plotted closest to the vertical axis. The resulting chart should look like this.

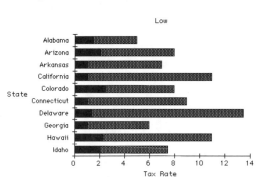

If you get rid of the first segment in each bar, you will have what appears to be a range bar chart. Position the pointer over any one of the black segments and click the mouse button. A white dot appears in three of the leftmost segments. You can now choose Patterns from the Format menu and make both the Area and Border Pattern of the selected segments Invisible.

All that is left to do is add a proper title, clean the chart up a bit, and frame it.

148

The Sliding Bar Chart

Each bar in a sliding bar chart represents all of some item, distributed between two major categories (each of which can be subdivided). The bar slides across a vertical base line, with one category extending on each side to show the relative proportion of the whole attributable to that category.

As with the other formats we have looked at, there are several different ways to create this format. One method is to overlap a positive and a negative series, as you did to create the floating column chart in Chapter 5. Another method makes more use of the MacPaint program, though it still uses Chart to establish the proportional relationship between two series. This example demonstrates the second method.

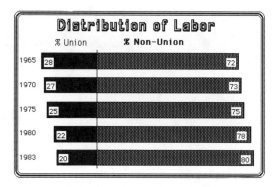

This chart shows how the distribution of union and non-union members has varied in the American labor force between 1965 and 1983. If you think of the chart as a segmented 100-percent bar chart on which some of the bars have been slid to the right so the breaking point between segments is in alignment for all bars, you will have an idea of the method by which this chart was created. Here are the numbers to be plotted.

Union			Non-Union		
Order: 1			Order: 2		
⊠ Plot Series			⊠ Plot Series		
year	percent		year	percent	
1983	20		1983	80	
1980	22		1980	78	
1975	25		1975	75	
1970	27		1970	73	
1965	28		1965	72	

Though we are working with dates, they do not represent equal time intervals, so you have to use a text series and type in the dates.

After creating the series and filling in the numbers, select format number 5—a segmented 100-percent bar chart—from the Bar Chart Gallery and click the Plot Series box in each series window. The series window you click first is plotted as the darker segment at the left end of each bar, and provides the title for the chart. As you can see from this illustration, I clicked the Union series first.

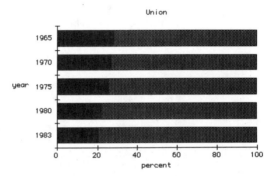

This is all we are going to do with the Chart program for this example; Chart has accurately established the proportional relationship between the union and non-union workers. I will now lead you on a quick excursion into the MacPaint program. I realize that MacPaint is not scheduled for discussion until Chapter 11, but I also know that it is not possible for a person to own a Macintosh and not use and enjoy MacPaint. So you might as well start applying it to enhancing charts, and therefore have an excuse for doing the playing you would do anyway.

Transferring a chart to MacPaint is not difficult; as with most other things, there are several methods. We will use the Clipboard to make this transfer. With the chart window on top of the other windows on your desktop, choose Copy Chart from the Edit menu. A dialog box appears, asking if you want the chart as it is shown on the screen, or as it would be shown when printed. The difference is that when you send a chart to the printer, its size and shape may be changed to fit the margins you set in the Page Setup dialog box. For this example, simply OK the preselection of As Shown on Screen. The disk drive hums for a moment as an image of the chart is stored in a Clipboard file. If you would like reassurance that something actually happened during all that humming, choose Show Clipboard from the Edit menu; the Clipboard appears, as in this illustration, and displays a small version of the chart you have just copied from the chart window.

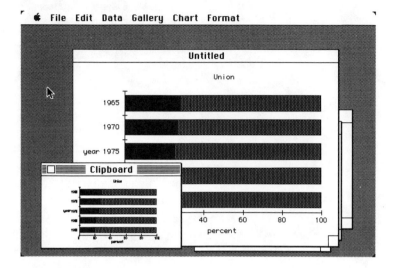

You can now quit the Chart program by choosing Quit from the File menu. If you haven't saved the chart since the last change, you are given the chance to do so before the program returns you to the Macintosh desktop.

Once back at the Macintosh desktop, close the Chart disk window, eject the disk, insert a disk with MacPaint on it, open its disk icon, and start the MacPaint program.

When the clean canvas appears, surrounded by its palette of patterns and tray of tools, choose Paste from the Edit menu, and the chart you copied to the Clipboard reappears.

One at a time, surround each bar below the top one with the selection rectangle and drag it to the right until the break between the segments lines up with that on the top bar (if you hold the Shift key down while dragging the bar, the bar's movement will be constrained to purely horizontal, vertical, or diagonal directions, making alignment easier).

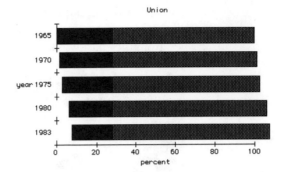

Your chart should now look like this. You could move the value scale to the right until the 0-percent tick mark lines up with the break, and then duplicate a few sections of axis under the Union bars, but it is more accurate to erase the axes entirely and type each bar's value on the bar itself. Add a title, a couple of subtitles, a line stressing the breaking point, and a frame, and you're done. With a little practice, the whole project can be completed in less than ten minutes.

One of the many strong points of the Macintosh is the way its programs relate to each other. You can easily pass information between programs, as we have just done between Chart and MacPaint, and can very quickly learn to use the special capabilities of one program to supplement and enhance another. More is said about MacPaint and several other Macintosh programs in Chapter 11.

The
Line
Graph

The identification of cause and effect relationships is critical to all types of planning—from playing the stock market to interpreting census information. The line graph, also known as the curve chart, is an extremely effective method of presenting large amounts of quantitative information in a form that allows the reader to quickly and easily recognize trends and relationships. The fluctuation of the line indicates the variations in the trend, while the distance of the line from the horizontal axis at any given point indicates a quantity. Placing multiple lines on the same axes or several line graphs on the same page enables you and your audience to evaluate information rapidly and to form an opinion about relationships.

The primary purpose of a line graph is either to depict trends over a period of time, or to show the relative distribution of one variable (such as test scores) throughout another variable (such as the student body).

Line graphs typically have more points to plot than the formats we have investigated so far and are especially efficient when there is considerable information to evaluate, as in following the daily closing price of a stock for a month.

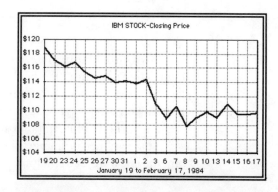

Your first concern when creating a line graph, as with any other graphic, should be to determine its purpose. The same information can be presented in a variety of ways, and used to prove a variety of points. If you are going to take the time to create a graph, make sure you present the information in a manner that is to your advantage.

As an example, here is a table of values and two graphs. One graph displays the values directly, the other shows the percentage of change by indexing on the first year plotted. Assuming that you represent management arguing against a pay raise for labor, which graph would you want to use?

Year	Wages	Profits
1980	100	10
1981	110	9
1982	112	8
1983	105	13
1984	115	18

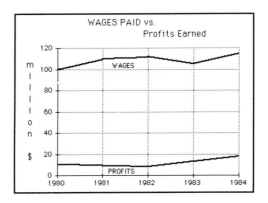

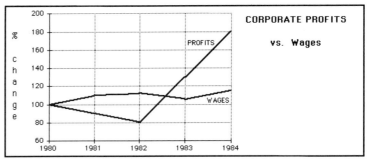

The idea for this example came from an illuminating book by Darrell Huff: *How to Lie with Statistics*. Contrary to the implication of its title, the book's purpose is to educate the public about the methods of graphic deception commonly used to prove a point that isn't necessarily true.

Thumbing through financial reports, you probably see more varieties of line graphs than of all other formats combined. They are extremely popular with economic forecasters and other such sayers of sooth. Most of the variations can be created by simply modifying one of Chart's standard formats.

As usual, you need to be concerned about a few standards, but you should be happy to have such concerns. There was no need to be aware of design techniques with earlier computerized graphing programs because you could not vary their formats; all you could change were the values to be plotted. With Chart you have gained the huge advantage of flexibility in exchange for a little extra thought on your part.

The Simple Line Graph

The primary—almost exclusive—use of line graphs is for plotting variations in value or frequency of occurrence. Amounts are scaled along the vertical Y-axis and time intervals are scaled along the horizontal X-axis. The label (such as Year or Month) for the time-interval axis can be omitted if the interval labels (1982, 1983) adequately describe the span; otherwise center a concise label beneath the axis.

When preparing your line graph, it is best to either omit grid lines completely or keep them to a minimum and draw them lightly, so that they do not compete for attention with the plotted line of the graph.

The Multiple Line Graph

More than one series can be graphed on the same axes; up to five lines can usually be deciphered without too much difficulty. When putting multiple lines on one chart, either use a different thickness or pattern for each line or mark each line with a unique symbol, so that it can be distinguished from the others and from the background.

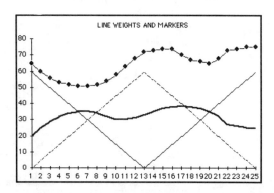

Each line should be labeled clearly, either adjacent to the line or with a legend that associates each line's symbol with the series it represents.

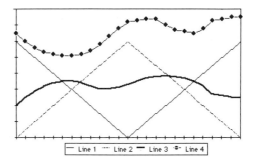

If an arrow is used to connect label and line, make it light and at a right angle to the line. Keep arrows away from line cross-over points to avoid confusion.

The High-Low Chart

The high-low chart (called HiLo by some newer business books and by Chart) is a specialized hybrid of the line graph, popularized primarily by the weekly plottings of the Dow Jones Industrial Average and other stock market trends.

The high-low chart is created by plotting the points of two or more series and then, instead of drawing a horizontal line connecting all the points in each series as you would for a multiple line graph, drawing a vertical line for each time interval from the highest series to the point directly below it on the lowest series. This dropline indicates the range of values at that particular time interval. A symbol is often placed at each end of the dropline to identify which series is associated with the high point and which with the low.

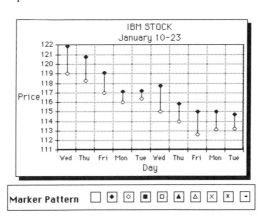

You can place additional symbols between the high and low points to indicate the average, the closing point, or some other significant piece of information. The Chart program provides a choice of the nine symbols displayed below this chart, or you can transfer your chart to the MacPaint program and create your own significant symbol.

The most common use of the high-low chart format is to compare the maximum-to-minimum ranges of sets of variables through a sequence of equal time intervals. When used in this manner, it is not necessary to label the horizontal axis; the unit labels are sufficient indication of the time period involved.

Multiple Graphs on One Page

When your multiple line graph starts looking like a can of worms (or maybe even a little sooner), it's time to divide before conquering. As many as 20 miniature graphs can be displayed on one page, each bearing its own bit of information.

If you expect somebody to compare these tidbits, keep the scales the same throughout, or at least group similar scales together. Also be consistent in the symbols you use; if you use a dotted line for a line projected into the future on one graph, don't use the same kind of line for some other purpose on another graph.

To place multiple graphs on one page, first create and save them one at a time, then use the MacPaint program, described in Chapter 11, to arrange them to suit your needs.

The Indexed Line Graph

Sometimes you may want to compare items that are so different in magnitude that they simply won't fit on the same scale. At other times you may want to compare things that are measured in different kinds of units, such as personal income (dollars) and wine consumption (gallons), or Apple Macintoshes and McIntosh apples.

Both kinds of comparison can be made with an indexed line graph, which is a graph of the variations in the value of an item compared with its value at a specific time. Economists use these graphs to express income and expenditures in constant dollars (which take into account the effects of inflation) instead of current dollars (which do not).

Indexed line graphs allow you to compare trends and examine the possibility of a relationship between two or more series. However, similar fluctuations in the activities of two items don't necessarily indicate that one is dependent on the other, or even that they are both dependent on a common factor.

Indexing a table

To convert the values in a series to indexed values, select a base year and divide each value by the value for that year. This procedure obviously gives you a quotient of one for the base year, a decimal value less than one for all years that have a value less than that of the base year, and a decimal value greater than one for those years with a value greater than that of the base year. Multiplying these quotients by 100 gives you a new set of values indexed to the selected base year. This table illustrates the indexing process.

	Values	Values divided by value of base year	quotient times 100
base year	2200	1.00	100
	2250	1.02	102
	2300	1.05	105
	2400	1.09	109
	2600	1.18	118
	2700	1.23	123
	2875	1.31	131

Applying this principle to the plotting of personal income, in dollars, versus wine consumption, in gallons, yields a graph such as this.

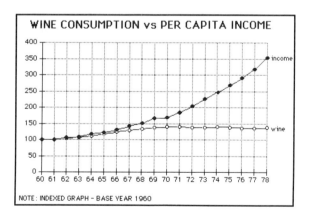

Both lines can be contained on the same axes, and the relationship between them is apparent. Most of this information was derived from a graph that plotted per capita income and total gallons of wine sold in the United States. This graph was produced by a liquor distributor, and the implication was that wine consumption was increasing at practically the same rate as per capita income—which may have been the case, but the cause is more likely attributable to the increase in the proportion of the population that is of drinking age than to any increase in income.

Choosing the base year

The year you choose as the base year for indexing can be a critical factor in the appearance of your finished graph. The most honest portrayal of a relationship is obtained by indexing on a normal year, though the meaning of "normal" depends a lot on what you're graphing. A good starting point is a year when the series was not going through dramatic change.

If you want to try other base years after indexing on one, the new values can be computed by dividing each value in the old indexed series by the value of the new base year.

The base line

Although not considered proper with most other formats, with an indexed line graph you can start the value scale at a level other than zero. Often you will need only a range of the scale sufficient to accommodate fluctuations of the trend around the 100 mark, 100 being the value at the base year.

The Multiple-Scale Line Graph

The multiple-scale line graph is a slightly less acceptable method of comparing two series that differ greatly in magnitude or unit of measure—less acceptable at least to those people who like clarity and ease of understanding.

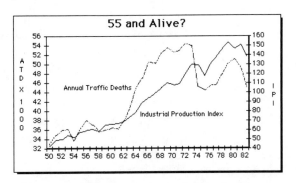

With such an explicit name, there is really little to explain, except that this graph format has scales on both the right and left sides and lines that relate to each. The primary concern is labeling; there should be no misunderstanding as to which label defines the value of which line.

The Logarithmic-Scale Line Graph

If you're hell-bent on confusion and nothing but the best is good enough for you, try the log graph—the line graph on a logarithmic scale.

Fortunately, you don't have to dredge up what you supposedly learned about logarithms in freshman math. The computer can take care of all the technical details, so invoking this format is no more difficult than selecting the correct option.

The primary purpose of the log scale is to compare the rate of change of multiple lines measured in unlike units. The significant difference between an arithmetic and a logarithmic scale is that on an arithmetic scale the distance between scale divisions is the same from the zero base line to the top of the scale, whereas on a logarithmic scale (as you see below) the numeric divisions stay the same but the distance between them decreases as you go up the scale (and the scale extends repetitively from 1 to 10, or multiples thereof).

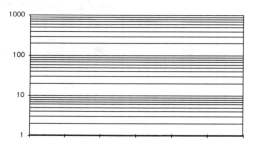

Charts that use the log scale on just one axis (usually the vertical one) are called semilogarithmic (semilog) charts; those that use it on both axes are called log-log charts.

The result of this unique method of scaling is that a straight line on a logarithmic chart represents a constant *rate* of change; a straight line on an arithmetic chart represents a constant *amount* of change. Here is an illustration of the same kinds of change plotted on the two scales.

ARITHMETIC   LOGARITHMIC

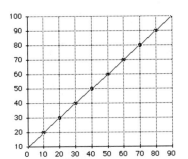 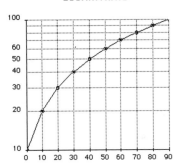

Constant Amount of Change

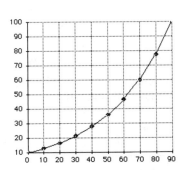 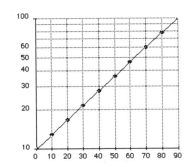

Constant Rate of Change

Creating Line Graphs

A line is defined in math books as *the path traced by a moving point.* When you create a line graph by hand, you mark the known data points in the plot area, place the point of your pencil on the first one, and trace a path to the next, and the next, and the next, and so on.

Although it would be possible to create a line graph with only one known data point at each end, such a graph would be deceptive, as the implication of a line graph is that the line represents the values between plotted points. The value at any point on the line can be estimated by drawing a line parallel to the X-axis that both passes through the unknown point and intersects the Y-axis. The point of intersection with the Y-axis represents the value of the unknown point. The closer together the known points are, the higher the likelihood of an accurate interpretation of the unknown point, as the following graph shows.

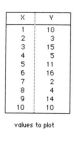

values to plot

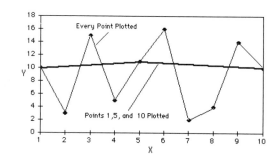

The Simple Line Graph

The first line graph we will plot gives us another look at how the government manages to spend our money; specifically, at how the amount of money spent by members of Congress for *free* franking (postage) varies from year to year. The information for this graph was extracted from annual editions of the *Budget of the United States Government*, released by the Government Printing Office.

The chart you create in this section should end up looking like this one.

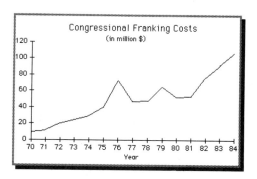

Creating a series

The first step toward creating a series (I'll assume from now on that you have cleared the screen of any old charts) is selecting the type and assigning a name and a few other properties. In this case the appropriate type is Date, because the values vary over a time period that is measured in equal increments.

Choosing Date from the Data menu displays this properties sheet and allows you to assign series, category, and value names. The series name, Congressional Franking Costs, will appear as the title for the graph. Chart automatically computes the category labels based on the First Category, Increment, and date unit you enter here.

```
┌─────────────────────────────────────────────────┐
│  Date Series                                       │
│                                                    │
│  Series Name:    ┌──────────────────────────────┐ │
│                  │ Congressional Franking Costs  │ │
│  Category Name:  ┌──────────────────────────────┐ │
│                  │ Year                          │ │
│  Value Name:     ┌──────────────────────────────┐ │
│                  │ Millions of Dollars           │ │
│                                                    │
│  First Category: ┌──────────────────────────────┐ │
│                  │ 1970                          │ │
│  Increment Each Category By                        │
│  ┌─────────┐                                       │
│  │ 1       │   ◉ Years ○ Months ○ Days ○ Weekdays │
│  └─────────┘                                       │
│                          ┌────────┐  ┌──────────┐  │
│                          │   OK   │  │  Cancel  │  │
│                          └────────┘  └──────────┘  │
└─────────────────────────────────────────────────┘
```

After filling in the properties sheet, click the OK button at the bottom; you are presented with a series window into which you can enter your data.

Entering data

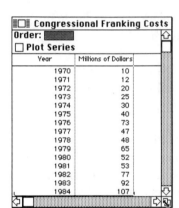

To enter the numbers to be charted, simply type them as they appear in the right column of this series window. The program will supply the date.

The date is presented in a format that is as close as possible to that which you used to enter the First Category on the Date Series properties sheet. If you would like the date to appear in another format, you can choose Categories from the Format menu and click the appropriate boxes.

You want this information plotted as a line graph, so choose Line from the Gallery menu. Click icon number 2, the closest format to the chart we want to create.

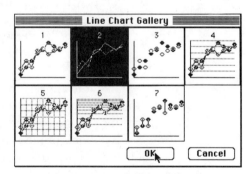

You can now return to the series window and click the Plot Series box. The graph that appears in the chart window should resemble the one that follows.

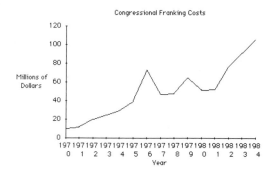

If your chart looks drastically different, check the numbers you entered. To correct a number, select it by either dragging the pointer through the amount or double-clicking it, and type the correct number.

Modifying the graph

A few minor manipulations with the mouse will transform the graph you have just produced into the one displayed at the beginning of this section.

First, let's eliminate the value-axis title (Millions of Dollars) and insert a subtitle (in million $) below the main title. This subtitle provides the same information while leaving room for the graph to expand.

To remove the value-axis title, select it (point and click), drag through the text to highlight it, and then choose Clear from the Edit menu. Millions of Dollars disappears instantly (kind of like government spending).

Display the main title in a larger size by selecting it and then choosing Text from the Format menu and clicking Medium under Font Size. To fit the larger title on one line, drag one of the end markers to make the insertion box longer.

Now insert the subtitle by clicking the spot where you would like it to appear, and typing it. The subtitle (in million $) appears within a frame of black handles. Varying the size of the subtitle's frame (by dragging a handle) controls how the text is displayed; it is printed on lines the width of the frame. If you would like to move the inserted text, position the pointer on the frame between handles (the pointer changes to a four-headed arrow to indicate the directions the frame can be moved) and drag it to its new location (by pressing the mouse button and moving the pointer).

Now let's turn our attention to the category axis, and do something to stop the labels from piling up on top of each other. There are several ways to solve this problem: You can enlarge the chart by enlarging the chart window, then selecting the chart and dragging one of the side handles; you can eliminate alternate tick labels by selecting the axis, choosing Axis from the Format menu, and entering 2 in the box for Number of Categories Between Tick Mark Labels; or you can click the Congressional Franking series window to bring it to the top, choose Categories from the Format menu, and click Short for Date Format. I chose the last method for my chart.

All that you have left to do is frame the graph—a task you should be familiar with by now. Choose Select Chart from the Chart menu and then Patterns from the Format menu to get this dialog box, which allows you to set the border pattern, weight, and style.

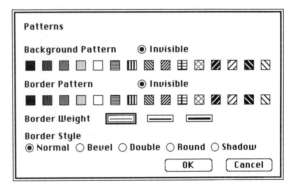

Try a few combinations; remember, the power of this program is that you can try various formats before picking the one you want to present to your audience.

Every graph should have a purpose; a typical purpose is to help you discover the relationships that exist between different events (represented by groups of numbers). Another purpose is to illustrate this relationship so that others can understand it. The graph you have just created is informative, and indicates that the cost of keeping congressmen in touch with their constituents is increasing; however, with inflation almost all costs are increasing, so this fact isn't really newsworthy. The interesting points on this graph are the sharp jumps that occur every four years. Do congressmen really have more to say to their constituents during election years? Or is the taxpayer simply subsidizing door-to-door delivery of political propaganda? If, as the creator of this graph, this is the view you would like to promote, then a subtle indication of the years during which elections are held would be appropriate.

One way to provide this indication is to insert a legend that identifies the election years. The resulting chart would look like this.

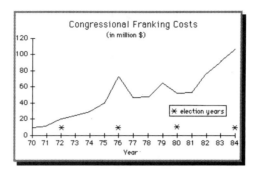

The Multiple Line Graph

You could add more lines to this same graph by repeating the steps used to create the first line, filling out a properties sheet and entering data in a series window for each line you want to add. If you add lines in this manner, the series type, first category, increment, unit, and number of data points should be identical, to allow accurate comparisons between series.

Category and value names should also be entered accurately; although the axes titles on the chart are taken from the first series plotted, you may later change the order of plotting. Also, the series name you assign on each properties sheet is used in the legend, so you should compose this title with clarity and conciseness in mind.

Rather than typing several new sets of numbers to illustrate the creation of a graph with multiple lines, let's allow the Chart program to create several new series based on its analyses of the series you entered for the Congressional Franking graph.

Analyzing the trend and growth

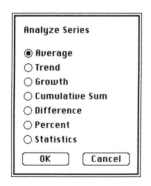

Selecting a series window and then choosing Analyze from the Data menu presents you with this list of the types of analysis available.

Clicking one of these selections causes the program to create a new series by feeding the data points of the currently selected series through formulas for growth, trend, average, and so on. A new properties sheet and series window are created, without disturbing the originals from which they were derived.

This new series is automatically linked to the original, so any change you make in the original is reflected in the new series. (To break the link, select the linked series window and then choose Unlink from the Edit menu.)

Let's apply the Trend and the Growth commands from this list to the Congressional Franking Costs series and plot the results. Click Trend, and then OK; another series window, labeled Trend of Congressional Franking, is created. Because the original series is plotted, the newly created series is automatically plotted; if you analyze a series that is not plotted, the result also is not plotted.

The plotted result of this analysis is a straight line that smooths out the fluctuations in Congressional spending for postage, and indicates the general direction in which this expenditure is moving: up.

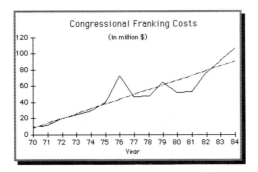

To add the growth curve to the chart, again select the Congressional Franking series window, choose Analyze from the Data menu, and click Growth. Another series and a new chart spring to life on your desktop.

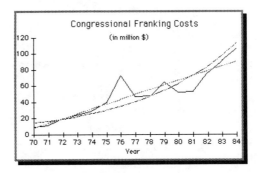

The newest line on the chart is a curve indicating the rate at which spending for postage is changing; the steeper the curve, the faster the change.

Modifying the graph

The only modification the chart really needs is some way to tell which line stands for what. The obvious way to do this is with a legend, but if you just choose Add Legend from the Chart menu, you will get a legend with some extremely long names (Trend of Costs of Congressional Franking). These names are taken from the series properties sheets, so if you select each series, bring up its properties sheet (choose Date from the Data menu), and shorten the series name, you will have a much more manageable legend.

You will also want to assign different weights to the lines by selecting each one, choosing Patterns from the Format menu, and clicking a pattern, weight, or marker.

Changing the name of the first series to improve the legend also changed the title for the chart. You will probably want to restore the original title by selecting the current one (Cost) and typing the old one (Congressional Franking Costs).

The only problem left to solve is the subtitle; since it is unattached text, it stayed in its previous position when the chart was redrawn—unlike the attached titles that remained centered on the plot area. Fortunately, it is easy to select the subtitle and drag it to the spot you want it. When you've finished, your chart is redrawn to look like this.

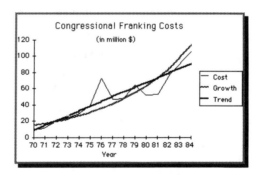

The High-Low Chart

When plotting a high-low chart, the only variation from the procedure used to produce a line graph is the obvious requirement that you have at least two series to plot. The Chart program *will* produce the plotted points of a single series, but this is a feat somewhat lacking in significance in a format designed to express the difference between points in two series.

To demonstrate the high-low format, we will create the following chart, plotting the high, low, and closing points for the Dow-Jones Industrial Average for the period from June 10 through 23, 1983. This task takes advantage of the Weekday unit of the Date series.

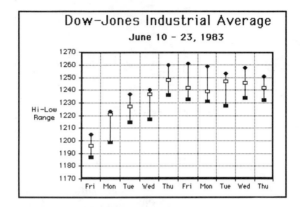

Creating a series

Choose Date from the Data menu to bring up a blank properties sheet. Fill in the sheet as I have this one, leaving the category name blank by entering a space or a backspace to eliminate Chart's preset title of X. As you can see in the above chart, the weekdays used for category labels on the chart adequately identify the axis. Since a category title is not going to be used, it is pointless to enter one and then later have to cut it out.

Chart accepts a variety of date formats; if you supply the month, day, and year, the program keeps track of the weekdays and supplies them on request. Click Weekdays for the date unit to instruct Chart to automatically provide the category labels of Monday through Friday, starting with the one that falls on the date you enter as First Category. Click OK on the Date Series properties sheet and choose Categories from the Format menu so you can tell Chart how to display the weekdays.

```
┌─────────────────────────────────────────────┐
│  Categories                                   │
│                                               │
│  Align              Show                      │
│  ○ Left             ☐ Year                    │
│  ○ Center           ☐ Quarter                 │
│  ● Right            ☐ Month                   │
│                     ☐ Day                     │
│  Date Format        ☒ Day of Week             │
│  ○ Short                                      │
│  ● Medium                                     │
│  ○ Long                                       │
│                                               │
│  Text Before: [_____]              │
│                                               │
│  Text After:  [_____]              │
│                                               │
│           [  ▶OK  ]    [ Cancel ]             │
└─────────────────────────────────────────────┘
```

Choosing Categories presents you with this dialog box. The options under Show determine which parts of the date are shown; clicking only Day of Week specifies that only the name of the days should appear. Clicking Medium under Date Format causes the days to be presented in an abbreviated form—Mon, Tue, and so on. (Clicking Short would result in M, T, clicking Long in Monday, Tuesday.

Since you know how you want your chart to appear, you can select these options before plotting it. If you are ever uncertain about the format to choose, draw the chart and try the different options; there are none that can't be undone either by going back to a dialog box and clicking the same one (to remove the X in its box), or by choosing a different option. If things get totally out of hand, you can choose New from the File menu (with the chart window selected) to reset the format to the basic column chart and start all over again.

Entering data

The series window you have created displays your series name in its top bar and the name Hi-Low Range above the value column, but there is no name above the category column because you left that box blank on the properties sheet.

When you type the high value for June 10, the word Fri, the day Chart determined June 10, 1983 fell on, appears on the top line of the category column.

When you type the next value, the word Mon appears (remember, Chart is supplying only weekdays). Continue

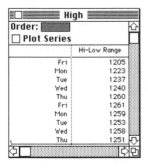

typing the values for each day, until your series window matches this one (I enlarged the window to display all the entries).

The second and third series

Rather than plotting just one series, let's enter the low values and the closing values and plot them all at the same time. The properties sheets for the next two series differ from that for the first only in their series names, Low and Closing.

Create each of these series and enter the values just as you did for the first series. Your series windows should end up looking like these.

Low			Closing		
Order:			Order:		
☐ Plot Series			☐ Plot Series		
		Hi-Low Range			Hi-Low Range
	Fri	1187		Fri	1196
	Mon	1199		Mon	1221
	Tue	1215		Tue	1227
	Wed	1217		Wed	1237
	Thu	1236		Thu	1248
	Fri	1233		Fri	1242
	Mon	1231		Mon	1239
	Tue	1228		Tue	1247
	Wed	1234		Wed	1246
	Thu	1232		Thu	1242

Converting from line to high-low

When you have finished filling in the numbers for all three series, you can chart them. Rather than choosing a high-low chart from the Line Chart Gallery, let's develop this chart through several stages by making use of the chart properties sheets available from the Chart and Format menus.

First, choose List from the Data menu and click the Plot boxes to specify that you would like all three series plotted. Assuming you are in the column chart format (the preset format when you start the Chart program), your plotted information will resemble this.

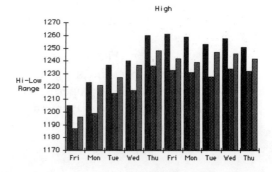

Now choose Main Chart Type from the Chart menu and click Line and OK. Your chart is redrawn like this one, which, as you can see, is beginning to bear some resemblance to the one we set out to duplicate.

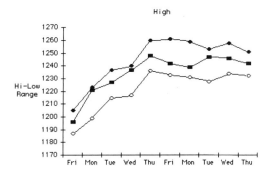

At any point you could choose number 7 from the Line Chart Gallery and have your presentation converted to a high-low variation of the line-graph format, but let's see if we can approach the same task through the back door. There will be times when you will need to construct charts that don't fit a stock format, so knowing how to manipulate chart properties sheets can be useful.

To change the properties associated with this chart, choose Main Chart from the Format menu. The Line Chart properties sheet has as one of its selections Hi-Lo Lines; click it and then click OK to see the result. It should look like this; we're getting even closer to our goal.

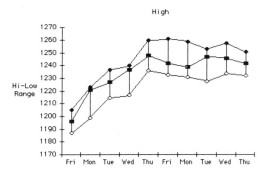

The only significant step left is eliminating the lines that connect the points in each series. Do this by returning to the Line Chart properties sheet you just left and clicking Lines Connecting Data Points to remove the X from the box. The chart is redrawn without the lines and this is the end result.

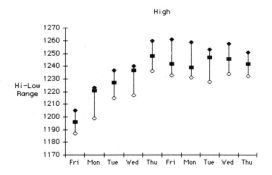

All that is left to do to this chart is apply the finishing touches and save it.

Changing symbols

A small item that can change the overall impression a chart makes on a reader is the choice of symbols to represent the data points plotted—the top, bottom, and middle of the high-low line. If you use a solid square for the low series, a solid diamond for the high series, and something hollow for the middle one, the overall impression is of an upward trend. Reversing the diamond and square gives the impression of a downward trend. Using hollow symbols for the endpoints and a solid one in the middle draws the eye to the middle, making that the most significant aspect. Try it and see.

To change the symbol used for the points in a series, select any point in the series (point and click). The first and last point in the series and one in the middle are marked with circles to indicate that the line and its points have been selected.

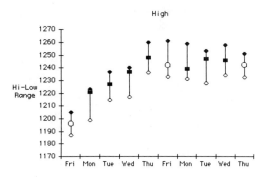

Now choose Patterns from the Format menu. The dialog box that appears offers you a choice of nine different marker patterns or none at all (a clear point).

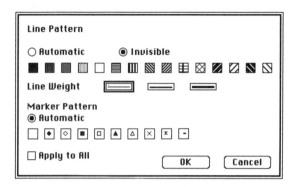

Click the symbol you would like to use, and then confirm your choice by clicking OK. Try different point combinations to see if your reaction to the chart is altered.

The Line Pattern portion of the above dialog box applies to the invisible lines connecting the points in each series; a different dialog box is presented if you select a hi-lo line and then choose Patterns from the Format menu.

Adding values

A chart such as the one we have just created can indicate a change and show the direction of a trend, but people who follow the Dow-Jones often desire a more accurate idea of the high, the low, or the closing than can be easily interpreted on a graph. This desire can be satisfied by appending to the chart the values that you previously entered into the series window. As a demonstration, let's add a value from the High series, say the third value, to the chart.

You append values as pieces of text. Click a blank spot on the chart and type any character (you can't choose the Format Text command unless some text is selected). Choose Text from the Format menu, then click Series or Data Point under Attached To and enter 1 in the Series Number box (High was the first series plotted) and 3 in the Point Number box. Click both Text and Size under Automatic, and Value under Show. When you return to the chart, the third value, 1237, appears above its plotted data point.

Text

Font
◉ Geneva   ☐ Italic
○ New York ☐ Bold
○ Chicago

Font Size
○ Small
◉ Medium
○ Large

Automatic
☒ Text
☒ Size

Show
☐ Key
☒ Value

Attached To
○ Unattached
○ Chart Title
○ Category Axis
○ Value Axis
◉ Series or Data Point

Orientation
◉ Horizontal
○ Vertical

Horizontal
Alignment
○ Left
◉ Center
○ Right

Vertical
Alignment
○ Top
◉ Center
○ Bottom

Series Number: [1]

Point Number: [3]

[OK]   [Cancel]

In this example we let the Chart program provide the attached value from the series window. You can provide a value or other text, and attach it in the same manner, by simply not clicking the Text box under Automatic on the Format Text properties sheet. The text you have selected will be attached to the specified data point. You should still click the Size box, so a space will be provided for the text.

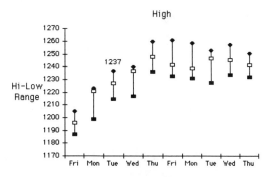

You have to repeat this process for each value you want to add. If you don't intend to modify the chart in the future, it is faster to transfer the chart to MacPaint and type the values in there. The advantage of doing the job in Chart is that you can change the values in the series window, or the shape or size of the chart, and the attached values are rewritten in the same position relative to their data points.

This chart can be quickly finished by adding grid lines (choose Axes from the Chart menu), framing the plot area (choose Select Plot Area from the Chart menu and Patterns from the Format menu), changing the title from High to Dow-Jones Industrial Average, and adding the appropriate subtitle.

The Indexed Line Graph

An indexed line graph displays the value of a variable relative to its value at some specific time. This specific time is known as the base period, and the value of the variable at that time is known as the base value.

What is an index number?

If you divide the current value of an item by its base value and multiply the resulting quotient by 100, the product is called the index number for that item (or the item index for the current time). The general formula is:

$$\text{index number} = \frac{\text{value}}{\text{base value}} \times 100$$

As an example, if I am paying $1.51 per gallon for gas in 1984 (which I am), and I were to look through the collection of charge slips in my glove compartment and discover that I was paying $.65 per gallon for the same kind of gasoline in 1977, the gasoline price index in 1984, with a base year of 1977, would be 232.31. The math looks like this:

$$\text{index number} = \frac{151}{65} \times 100 = 232.31$$

The Consumer Price Index

The best known index is the Consumer Price Index (CPI), which is published monthly by the Bureau of Labor Statistics. The CPI represents over 400 separate indices (such as our gasoline example), each assigned a weight to account for its relative importance in the budget of the average consumer.

This series window lists the CPIs from 1970 to 1982, with a base year of 1977. The graph beside it represents the same information.

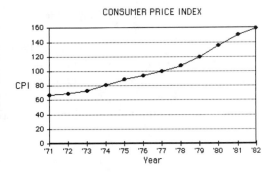

The index number for the base year is always 100 (in the base year the current value equals the base value; dividing one by the other yields a quotient of 1). If the current value increases, the plotted line slopes up; if the value decreases, the plotted line slopes down.

If you want to convert to a different base year (which changes the appearance of the graph), you divide the CPI for each year by the CPI for the new base year.

The CPI is often plotted as a second line on a graph to show how one item, such as wages, has varied with respect to the variation in the CPI, which represents the buying power of those wages. A second way to use the CPI is to convert current dollars (those we earn today) to constant dollars (the dollars we earned in the base year). The advantage of doing this is that the unit of measurement stays in dollars, which people are familiar with, rather than the CPI which is an abstract ratio that has no real meaning (though—as the CPI indicates—the dollar itself seems to have less and less real meaning). The formula for converting from current dollars to constant dollars is:

$$\text{constant dollars} = \frac{\text{current dollars}}{\text{current CPI}} \times 100$$

As an example, if your wages in 1977 were $12,000 and you thought you were doing better when, in 1982, you made $18,000, you would probably have second thoughts after converting those 1982 wages to constant dollars. Here is the math:

$$\text{constant dollars} = \frac{\$18,000}{159.0} \times 100 = \$11,321$$

The $18,000 you earned in 1982 had the buying power $11,320 had in 1977. In order to break even with inflation, you would have had to have made $19,080 in 1982 to maintain your 1977 buying power.

177

Plotting weekly wages

The previous discussion was a long lead-in for our next graph, which plots the change in the average weekly wages of production and nonsupervisory workers, on an annual basis, for the years from 1974 to 1982. One series plots each year's current dollars, and the other series plots constant dollars (with a base year of 1977).

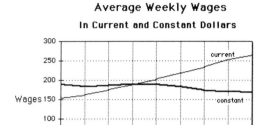

Average Weekly Wages
In Current and Constant Dollars

Since you are plotting values measured at equal time intervals, a date series is appropriate. Bring up a properties sheet for the first series by choosing Date from the Data menu.

You will create two series for this graph. The properties sheet for the first series should be filled out like the one shown here; for the second series just change the series name to Constant Dollars.

```
Date Series

Series Name:      Current Dollars
Category Name:    Year
Value Name:       Wages

First Category:   1974
Increment Each Category By

1          ⦿ Years  ◯ Months  ◯ Days  ◯ Weekdays

                            [ OK ▶ ]   [ Cancel ]
```

Enter the dollar amounts shown in the left series window into your first series window (the dates are supplied by the program), and then create another date series and enter the values from the right window.

Current Dollars		Constant Dollars	
Order: ▓▓▓▓		Order: ▓▓▓▓	
☐ Plot Series		☐ Plot Series	
Year	Wages	Year	Wages
1974	154.76	1974	190.12
1975	163.53	1975	184.16
1976	175.45	1976	186.85
1977	189	1977	189
1978	203.7	1978	189.31
1979	219.91	1979	183.41
1980	235.1	1980	172.74
1981	255.2	1981	170.13
1982	266.92	1982	167.87

You are now ready to plot all the points you have entered. Take a look at the Gallery menu and choose Line Chart, if it doesn't already have a check in front of it. Select icon number 2 and click OK. Now you can click Plot Series in both series windows and watch as your chart is drawn.

Modifying the chart

I'll leave to you the tasks of typing in a new title and adding a frame and grid. The only other change that I recommend is making the plotted lines a little heavier and adding a legend to tell which line is which.

To change the weight of a line, you first select the line by clicking it, and then choose Patterns from the Format menu and click a different weight.

To add a grid, choose Axes from the Chart menu and click Major Grid Lines under both Categories and Values.

The Multiple-Scale Line Graph

In order to change the frequency at which an event occurs, it is usually necessary to discover and then try to control the cause. The multiple-scale line graph is one convenient method of comparing events that are measured in different units to see if there is a possible relationship. Since effect often lags behind cause (as in the birth rate), it is often necessary to plot points for a long period to discover a relationship. The graph I have created to illustrate this section has a total of 66 data points (in two series), so you may want to just read along and take my word for it that things turn out as I say they do.

The concept for this creation came from an article in *Car and Driver* magazine. The article's author questioned crediting the 55 MPH speed limit with reductions in traffic fatalities. Although advocates of the 55 MPH speed limit have presented statistics and graphs "proving" their belief that the lower speed limit saves lives, the author maintains that they are only presenting part of the information. A more thorough investigation, he claims, reveals that the cause of variations in the death rate on America's highways is the attitude of drivers, which he feels is influenced by the current economic situation. A graph similar to this one was provided to "prove" his point.

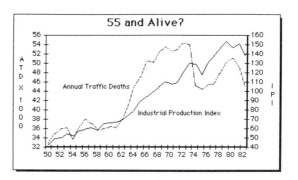

Creating the graph

To produce this graph you create two separate series, one for Annual Traffic Deaths and one for the Industrial Production Index, which is an indicator of the overall economic situation. You then overlay the chart for one with the chart for the other—just like projecting one overhead transparency on top of another for a composite picture. And just as with overlaying transparencies, you need a few points in common between the two graphs to make sure everything is aligned properly. The common points for these two graphs are the dates scaled along the horizontal axis—a scale created from the entries on the bottom lines of the properties sheet for each series.

```
┌─────────────────────────────────────────────────────┐
│ ┌─────────────────────────────────────────────────┐ │
│ │ Date Series                                       │ │
│ │                                                   │ │
│ │ Series Name:    ┌──────────────────────────────┐ │ │
│ │                 │ Annual Traffic Deaths        │ │ │
│ │                 └──────────────────────────────┘ │ │
│ │ Category Name:  ┌──────────────────────────────┐ │ │
│ │                 │ Year                         │ │ │
│ │                 └──────────────────────────────┘ │ │
│ │ Value Name:     ┌──────────────────────────────┐ │ │
│ │                 │ ATD X 1000                   │ │ │
│ │                 └──────────────────────────────┘ │ │
│ │                                                   │ │
│ │ First Category: ┌──────────────────────────────┐ │ │
│ │                 │ 1950                         │ │ │
│ │                 └──────────────────────────────┘ │ │
│ │ Increment Each Category By                        │ │
│ │ ┌──────────┐                                      │ │
│ │ │ 1        │  ◉ Years ○ Months ○ Days ○ Weekdays │ │
│ │ └──────────┘                                      │ │
│ │                        ┌────────┐  ┌──────────┐  │ │
│ │                        │  OK    │  │ Cancel   │  │ │
│ │                        └────────┘  └──────────┘  │ │
│ └─────────────────────────────────────────────────┘ │
└─────────────────────────────────────────────────────┘
```

Fill in the first Date Series properties sheet as I did this one. On the second sheet change the series name to Industrial Production Index and the value name to IPI. The category name and the bottom two lines stay the same.

Here are the numbers to be plotted on this graph; the column headed ATD X 1000 is the number of annual traffic deaths in thousands, and the one headed IPI is the Industrial Production Index.

YEAR	ATD X 1000	IPI	YEAR	ATD X 1000	IPI
1950	33	33	1967	50.2	100
1951	35	49	1968	52.5	105
1952	36	50	1969	53.5	110
1953	36.2	55	1970	52.6	108
1954	33.7	52	1971	53	110
1955	36.3	58	1972	54.5	120
1956	38	60	1973	54	130
1957	37	61	1974	45.2	129
1958	35.5	58	1975	44.5	118
1959	36	65	1976	45.5	131
1960	36.4	66	1977	45.5	138
1961	36.1	67	1978	47.9	146
1962	38	70	1979	50.3	153
1963	41	75	1980	51.1	147
1964	45	80	1981	49.3	151
1965	47.1	90	1982	45	138
1966	50.5	95			

As you type the numbers into a series window, they start scrolling off the top of the column when you get to 1955. Remember that you can review your entries by enlarging the window or by using the scroll bar along the right side.

If you are an energetic nonbeliever and actually typed all those numbers, the next step is plotting the charts. As with other charts in other formats, there is more than one way to plot overlaid charts. You could, for example, choose Main Chart Type and then Overlay Chart Type from the Chart menu, click Line in each dialog box, and then move the vertical axis for the overlay chart to the right end of the horizontal axis. However, if you look at the Combination Chart Gallery, you will see an easier method of achieving the same results.

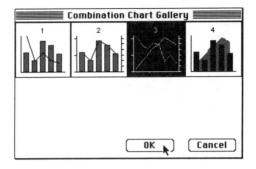

Selection number 3 in this gallery is a combination line chart with main and overlay charts, each with a separate scale. Select this format, which is very close to the format we are trying to create, and then plot both series (Annual Traffic Deaths first). This chart is produced.

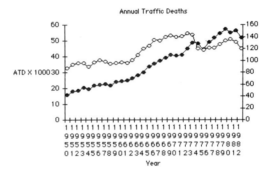

You now have a chart in the correct format but rather crowded. Moreover, it tells you very little about the relationship between traffic deaths and the Industrial Production Index. The steps required to make this chart presentable are all simple things you have done before on other charts. Here is a set of steps for the first few changes.

- Click the Annual Traffic Deaths series window to bring it to the top, choose Categories from the Format menu, and click Short for Date Format.

- Click the chart window to bring it to the top, select the horizontal axis, choose Axis from the Format menu, and enter 2 in the box after Number of Categories Between Tick Mark Labels.

- Select the main chart value axis (vertical axis on left), choose Axis from the Format menu, and set Minimum to 32, Maximum to 56, and Major Unit to 2.

■ Select the overlay chart value axis (vertical axis on right), choose Axis from the Format menu, and set Minimum to 40 and Major Unit to 10 (leave Maximum as it is).

If you followed these steps, the chart on your desktop should now look like this one.

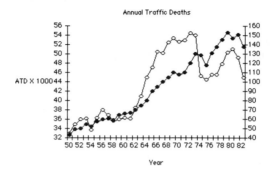

The next set of steps changes each piece of text on the chart and removes the markers from both lines.

■ The chart title should be 55 and Alive? so select the chart title, Annual Traffic Deaths, and change it.

■ While the new main title is still selected, choose Text from the Format menu and click Bold and Large in the Font section.

■ Select the main chart value-axis title (ATD X 1000), choose Text from the Format menu, and click Vertical under Orientation.

■ Select the category-axis title (Year), and remove it by choosing Clear from the Edit menu.

■ Add the title IPI to the overlay value axis by clicking near it and typing the title. Orient the title vertically, just as you did the main chart value-axis title.

■ Remove the line markers by selecting a marker on one line, choosing Patterns from the Format menu, and clicking both the blank pattern and Apply to All. Repeat this process for the other line.

■ Add the labels Annual Traffic Deaths and Industrial Production Index, each adjacent to the appropriate line.

Your chart should now look like this one, which lacks only a frame around the plot area and around the chart.

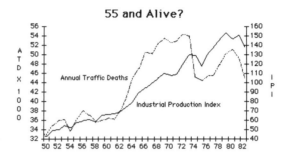

To frame the plot area, choose Select Plot Area from the Chart menu and then choose Patterns from the Format menu and click the black border pattern. To frame the chart, choose Select Chart from the Chart menu and again choose Patterns from the Format menu. Click both the black border pattern and the shadow frame style.

The Logarithmic-Scale Line Graph

I may have been a little disparaging of the log graph in my earlier discussion of line graph standards; it is an unusual format and one that is sometimes difficult for the uninitiated to understand. An important point I should make regarding logarithmic graphs is that with the Chart program, there is no need to understand logarithms in order to use this format.

The primary purpose of the logarithmic graph is to compare the rate of change of variables expressed in different units or in units of different magnitude. An example of the latter would be the comparison of the crime rate in a specific city, or in several cities of different size, to the crime rate for the nation.

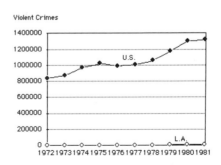

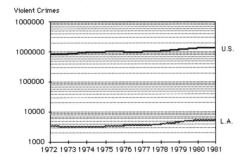

These graphs compare the number of violent crimes committed each year in Los Angeles, from 1972 through 1981, with the number committed throughout the country during the same period. Both graphs plot the same information, the one on the left with an arithmetic scale and the one on the right with a semilog scale. The difference in magnitude is so great that on the arithmetic chart, a scale that includes the number of crimes in the U.S. barely shows the number in Los Angeles. The logarithmic scale, on the other hand, allows a comparison of the rate of change, even though the numbers are vastly different.

There is nothing tricky about creating a graph in this format; you simply create the appropriate series, enter the data, and choose icon number 6 from the Line Chart Gallery.

The
Pie
Chart

The pie chart is a format that is universally recognized and understood. It is impossible to express a complex relationship with a pie chart; it cannot compare multiple series, it should not present more than eight or ten data points, and there are no fancy logarithmic scales available for it.

In the first part of this chapter, I will discuss the standards that apply to this simple format. The restrictions on the construction of pie charts are not severe, but the few that do exist are important.

Standards

A pie chart (sometimes called a sector chart) is used to compare the relative proportions of the parts that make up the whole. The circular pie represents all there is, and the size of each sector shows its share. The arrangement of the sectors allows you to compare them to each other as well as to the whole. Although the exact value of each segment is more difficult for the reader to interpret with pie charts than with bar charts, the relationship to the whole is more obvious.

The Simple Pie Chart

Give some thought to your audience when you consider the pie chart as a means of conveying information. Since it is so simple, sophisticated viewers often ignore it, assuming the information it presents to be insignificant.

Pie charts such as this are often used by public organizations to explain to the people supporting them just how they spent their money. Bureaucrats seem to feel more comfortable showing you the percentage of their budget allocated to each expense area rather than the dollar amount actually spent, though for clarity both pieces of information should be available someplace on the chart.

The restrictions on the construction of pie charts are more to avoid clutter than to facilitate accurate interpretation. Adhering to the following guidelines helps you produce a pie you can be proud to serve.

Number of segments

The number of pieces into which you can cut your pie is influenced by the final size of the displayed chart, which is not necessarily the size it appears in the Macintosh's chart window. Twelve segments are usually considered the practical limit and eight are common; but five or six is the optimum number.

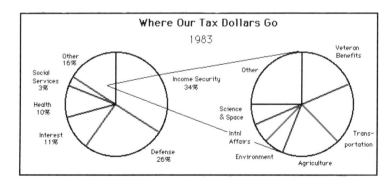

Often, as shown here, you can combine similar categories and show a component breakdown with a separate chart in order to reduce the number of segments to a reasonable level.

Placement of segments

Unlike the portions of pie dished up at your favorite restaurant, the individual pieces of a pie chart usually vary substantially in size. The normal method of arranging these slices, as shown in the last two illustrations, is from largest to smallest, in a clockwise direction starting at zero degrees (12 o'clock). If you group small segments together to form a "miscellaneous" or "all other" category, place this combination segment after all others, regardless of its cumulative size.

When several segments are similar in size and it is difficult to interpret relationships accurately, include with each segment its value or the percentage of the whole it represents.

Exploding the pie chart

As I demonstrated with the sample pie chart in Chapter 2, exploding the pie is not as drastic (or as messy) as it sounds; it is simply a method of emphasizing one or more segments by moving them away from the center of the pie. The Chart program allows you to control the position of each segment individually, permitting charts like this one.

Shading

Shading is another method of emphasis available with a pie chart. The usual warning about patterns applies; progress from dark to light in a clockwise direction, starting with the first segment at 12 o'clock.

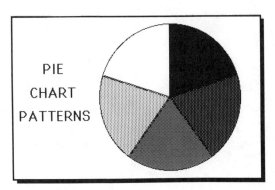

The primary purpose of patterns on a pie chart is to provide distinctive identifying symbols to be used in a legend. If you are not going to use a legend, consider also skipping the shading; a plain pie with no patterns to differentiate the segments allows you to place labels within each segment without creating clutter. If you do use patterns, avoid ones that clash.

Labels

Labels should be horizontal if possible, vertical if necessary; but under no circumstance should they radiate out from the center. If there is enough room, labels can be placed within the segments they refer to; otherwise, they should appear around the perimeter. If there is any doubt which segment a label refers to, use an arrow to make the connection.

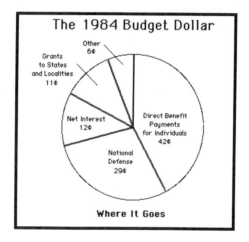

Legends

When your display becomes so cluttered with arrows that you suspect an Indian attack, allow Chart to help you clean up the mess with a legend (no, I don't mean Davy Crockett).

A chart legend is composed of a small sample of each pattern and its related label. The legend can be placed on the chart in a variety of formats and positions to make the chart more informative and to help balance the presentation.

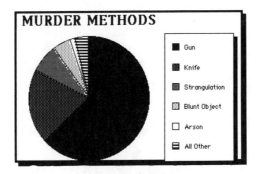

Presentation

Once you have the chart arranged in a manner that correctly and effectively displays the available information, give some thought to how you will present it to your reader. Consider its location within the text on the printed page or transparency, as well as the weight and balance of the individual components and of the chart as a whole.

Putting a rectangular or square frame around the pie visually ties it down to the page and helps maintain balance. Chart provides a variety of basic frames that you can use "as is" or you can move the chart to the MacPaint program and alter its frame for the desired effect.

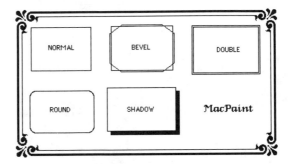

The Multiple Pie Chart

Since a pie chart always represents 100 percent of the category it is charting, only one series can be depicted by one pie. The relationship between several sets of numbers can be examined, however, by placing multiple pies on one chart.

Multiple pie charts normally use equal-sized, individual circles separated by a distance of approximately half the common diameter, with segment values identified as percentages instead of absolute numbers. Arrange the circles in a logical order, with an appropriate title, and identify each.

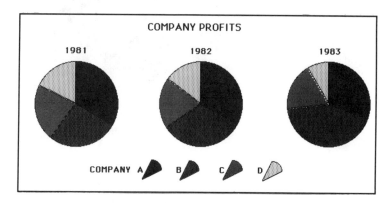

With multiple pie charts, the rule about starting the circle with the largest segment is overridden by the necessity to maintain the same order in each pie for easy comparison. The order and shading of all the pies should be governed by that of the first. This consistency in order allows you to either label the first pie, and let it serve as a key for the rest, or include a legend that applies to all the pies.

Creating Pie Charts

Creating a pie chart is quick and easy compared to other formats. You still have to fill out a properties sheet, but there are never many data points to plug in.

The Simple Pie Chart

For our first exercise in pie charting we will look at the methods of committing murder in the United States in 1979. The polished pie chart you end up with will resemble this one.

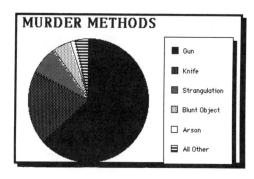

To produce this chart you first create a series, then enter information for six categories.

Creating a series

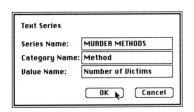

As usual, you should first clear any existing clutter from Chart's Desktop (if you are working on another chart, save it, and then choose New from the File menu).

Since this is a text series (guns, knives, and so on), choose Text from the Data menu and fill in the resulting Text Series properties sheet with the information shown.

Entering data

When you click OK on the properties sheet, a series window with the series, category, and value names you typed onto the properties sheet appears. Beneath the titles are two empty columns; since this is a text series, you have to enter information in both columns.

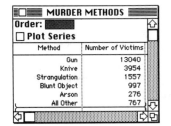

Type the first category label, Gun, in the left column, press Enter to move to the right column, type the value, and press Enter again. Repeat this process until you have entered all the information that appears in this series window.

After you have entered the six lines of information, click Plot Series to plot the points. Since you started this session by returning all formats to their preset conditions, a column chart is plotted. To select the pie format, choose Pie from the Gallery menu. You are presented with this platter of pies.

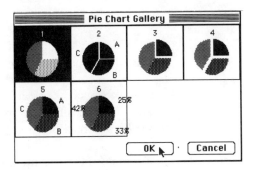

Style number 1 is a good starting point; select it by clicking its icon (the icon becomes highlighted), and then click the OK button at the bottom of the dialog box to confirm your choice and redraw the chart.

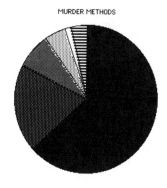

MURDER METHODS

This pie chart looks nice, but doesn't really tell us much; there is no indication of which method of mayhem each segment represents. Let's make a few changes to prepare this pie for presentation to the public.

Modifying the chart

The most obvious and easiest change is to add a legend identifying the segments. This is rapidly accomplished by choosing Add Legend from the Chart menu, which produces this more informative chart.

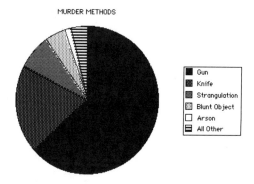

MURDER METHODS

Transforming this chart into the finished product involves several simple steps, which I will list here and leave for you to do if you want to.

- To balance the size of the pie, enlarge the legend by selecting it, choosing Legend from the Format menu, and clicking Medium under Spacing of Entries.

- While the legend is still selected, choose Patterns from the Format menu and click the Shadow border style.

- Give the chart title a little more weight by selecting it and then choosing Text from the Format menu and clicking New York, Bold, and Large in the Font section.

- Frame the chart by selecting it (choose Select Chart from the Chart menu) and then choosing Patterns from the Format menu and clicking the black, heavyweight border in the shadow style.

That is all there is to it. You should now have a chart that looks just like the one we set out to create.

The Multiple Pie Chart

Although one pie chart cannot be used to express more than one series, multiple pie charts can be placed on the same page to allow the viewer to make comparisons.

The Chart program does not allow you to directly create multiple charts, but used in conjunction with the Mac-Paint program, described in Chapter 11, you can easily create multiple charts in any format. The first step of this process is the creation and storage of several charts.

Creating the first pie chart

In keeping with our present theme of murder and mayhem, we now turn our attention to the methods of suicide employed by males and females. The time period for this chart is the same year as the previous example: 1979.

Clear the Murder Methods chart from the work area and create two text series, named Male and Female. As you may have noticed on the last chart, the category and value names you enter on a series properties sheet don't appear on the pie chart; but they are handy to have in the series window, so go ahead and assign Methods and Number as the category and value names.

Male		Female	
Order: ▨		Order: ▨	
☐ Plot Series		☐ Plot Series	
Methods	Number	Methods	Number
Firearm	12919	Firearm	2639
Poison	2878	Poison	2754
Strangulation	2783	Strangulation	742
Other	1580	Other	815

The information to be entered into both series windows appears above. The left window shows the methods used by successfully suicidal males in our society, the right window gives the same information for females. Enter the numbers for the male-suicides series into its window, just as you did the information for the last chart.

After you have entered the information for the first series, copy the window's contents to the other series window (select all four lines, then choose Copy from the Edit menu, click the Female series window to select it, and choose Paste from the Edit menu). Change the numbers in the Female window to those shown above. Not only is copying the series easier

than typing the categories again, it ensures that the order stays the same, which is important with multiple-pie charts.

Plot the Male series first; choose number 5 from the Pie Chart Gallery and then click Plot Series to get this chart.

We need to move both this chart and the Female chart we are about to create to the MacPaint program to combine them into one chart. In Chapter 6 we moved a chart to MacPaint by copying it to the Clipboard, quitting Chart, starting the MacPaint program, and pasting the contents of the Clipboard onto the MacPaint work area. If we used the same method with this example, we would have to make two trips between Chart and MacPaint, as the Clipboard can only hold one item at a time. Instead, let's paste both charts into the Scrapbook, where they can both be stored indefinitely. After we finish this charting session, we can move a copy of the Scrapbook file to the disk holding the MacPaint program. The charts can then be brought out and used whenever needed.

To copy your chart to the Scrapbook, first copy it to the Clipboard, as you did in Chapter 6, by bringing the chart window to the top of the windows on your desktop and then choosing Copy Chart from the Edit menu. Once in the Clipboard, the chart can be pasted into the Scrapbook by choosing Scrapbook from the Apple menu and, when the Scrapbook window appears on your desktop, choosing Paste from the Edit menu. The disk drive hums a bit, and a copy of your chart appears in the Scrapbook. You can now click the close box in the corner of the Scrapbook window, return to the Chart program, and plot the next series.

Plot the Female chart by first clicking the Plot Series box in the Male series window to un-plot it, then clicking the Plot Series box in the Female chart. Although we won't end up using the labels (Firearms, Poison, and so on) on the Female chart, keep them for the initial plotting. The program automatically adjusts the size of each chart it draws to fill the space available in the chart window; without labels, the Female chart would be drawn to a larger scale to take up the room previously used by the labels. Though you can manually adjust the size of a chart after it is drawn, it is simpler to stick to the same format and have Chart draw the same size chart automatically; you can erase the labels after the chart is moved to MacPaint.

When this chart of suicide methods used by the gentler gender appears, copy it to the Scrapbook just as you did the chart for successfully suicidal males.

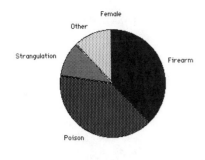

The pictures and text that you paste into the Scrapbook are stored by the Macintosh in a file that you can see on its desktop. This file, called the Scrapbook file, has an icon resembling a Macintosh, indicating it is a system file. You can move this file between disks, change its name, or throw it in the trashcan, just as you can a document file.

The easiest way to move your two charts into the MacPaint program is to move the Scrapbook file containing them to the MacPaint disk. Bear in mind when you make this move that only one file named Scrapbook can be on a disk at a time. If there is already a Scrapbook file on the MacPaint disk and you try to copy another one to the disk, an alert box appears asking if you would like to replace the existing file with the new file, effectively erasing the contents of the existing file. If you want to preserve the contents of the MacPaint disk's Scrapbook, temporarily rename it. When you are through with the new Scrapbook, you can throw it in the trashcan and change the name of the original file back to Scrapbook.

Combining your two pie charts in MacPaint takes only a few minutes and requires no artistic talent. Here are the steps to follow after transferring a copy of the Scrapbook file to the MacPaint disk.

■ Start the MacPaint program.

■ Open the Scrapbook window by choosing Scrapbook from the Apple menu.

■ Scroll through the Scrapbook until you find one of your pie charts.

■ Copy the chart to the Clipboard by choosing Copy from the Edit menu.

■ Close the Scrapbook window by clicking its close box.

■ Paste the contents of the Clipboard into the MacPaint work area by choosing Paste from the Edit menu.

■ Repeat the process for the other chart.

Once both charts are in MacPaint, you can erase unwanted parts, position them properly, frame the combination, and add a title. Errors in artistic judgment can be remedied with the Undo command or the eraser; extreme errors can be covered with another copy from the Scrapbook and a fresh start.

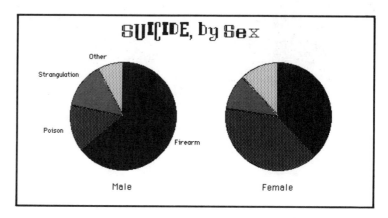

This is one way your chart could end up. The Mac-Paint program gives you precise control of the images you produce and manipulate; you would have no problem duplicating the chart I have created, but your own sense of taste and balance may lead you in other directions. Here are the steps I followed after copying the two charts from the Scrapbook.

■ Select the eraser by clicking its icon in the panel of tools at the left of the MacPaint desktop. When the pointer is moved to the work area, it takes on the shape of the eraser.

■ Remove the unwanted labels from around the Female chart by dragging the eraser over them.

■ Pick the selection rectangle from the panel of tools and drag it over the Female chart; drag the Female chart to where you would like it, relative to the Male chart.

■ Still using the selection rectangle, drag the chart titles, Male and Female, and position them beneath their respective charts.

■ To add a title, first click the A in the tool panel to let the program know you want to enter text, next click the spot you want the title to begin, and finally, type the title. Until you choose a different tool or click someplace else in the work area, you can backspace over the text you type (to make corrections), or change its font, fontsize, or style as often as you want.

■ Create a frame. The frame for this chart is larger than the work area, so it must be created in stages. You can move the chart around with the hand from the tool panel, and draw sections of line with the line-drawing tool. Drawing a horizontal or vertical line is easier if you hold the Shift key down while you drag the pointer to create the line.

That is all there is to combining two charts in Mac-Paint. After you have done it once, doing it with other charts will probably take less time than reading these instructions.

The
Area
Chart

This chapter starts with an explanation of the standards that apply to the creation of area charts, and then goes on to a step-by-step demonstration of how different styles of area charts are produced.

Standards

Although area charts, sometimes called surface or component band charts, occupy their own classification in the charting world, at one time or another they exhibit all the characteristics of both simple line graphs and stacked column charts.

The Simple Area Chart

Simple area charts such as this one appear frequently in magazines and newspapers; they catch the reader's eye and are easy to interpret.

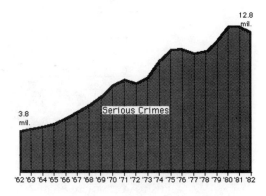

The simple area chart, like the simple line graph, is typically used to show variations in the value of an item over a period of time. An area chart that contains only a single series is plotted just like a line graph, the only noticeable difference between the two formats being that the area beneath the area chart's line is filled in with a pattern or an illustration to help identify the subject and emphasize the trend. The Chart program can provide its usual array of patterns and drop lines to decorate this format, or you can transfer the chart to the Mac-Paint program and fill in the area with your own artwork.

Since the area chart is typically used to show variations in value that are measured and labeled at regular and obvious time intervals (days, months, years), the horizontal axis, along which these intervals are marked, does not usually require a title. The interval names themselves (Sun, Mon, Tues, and so on) should be enough to identify the category to the reader.

Unless you are presenting your chart to a sophisticated audience, familiar both with this format and with the information being plotted, avoid starting the value scale from any point other than zero.

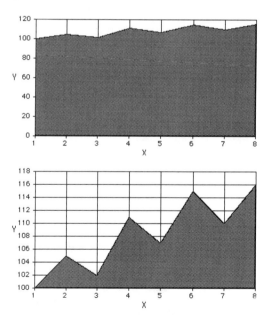

As these illustrations show, starting at a higher point tends to accentuate change, and therefore distort the information you are presenting.

The plotted line on an area chart should extend from the vertical axis on the left side of the chart to a point above the last interval marked on the horizontal axis on the right side. The shading beneath should also fill the entire area, from side to side. If you use drop lines to carry specific points on the plotted line down to the horizontal axis, they should be lighter in weight than the plotted line itself.

The Subdivided Area Chart

An area chart can be used to plot more than one series, in which case it exhibits the qualities of a stacked column chart. The different bands indicate the cumulative trend of more than one series or the component parts of a trend that was previously plotted as a single series. This is a good method of plotting multiple series when there are too many data points for a stacked column chart and when the values of each series are too close together to be easily discernible on a line graph.

Because the subdivided area chart appears to be a line graph with all the open areas filled in, there is sometimes confusion in its interpretation. Unlike a line graph, where every point on the line represents a numeric distance above or below the base line, the top of each band in an area chart indicates the sum of the value of that band and all the bands below it. Because the bands are cumulative, they can never cross—so converting to an area chart unclutters a line graph that has crisscrossed lines (known in graphing circles as the can of worms effect).

X	one	two
1	4	7
2	5	6
3	7	5
4	8	6
5	7	7
6	6	10
7	5	12

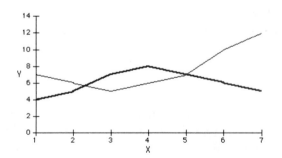 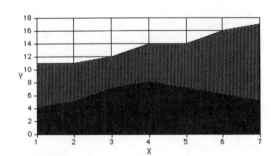

Placement of bands

The order of the bands, from bottom to top, should follow a logical progression.

One method of distributing the bands is by order of significance. Since the bottom band is the easiest to interpret, and is also normally the darkest and therefore the most conspicuous band, this position is usually reserved for the band that is most significant to you.

A second method, which makes the overall interpretation of the chart easier, is to place the most stable band on the bottom and work up through the less stable bands.

These two charts, which plot the same data, show how the appearance of a chart is changed when you change the order of the bands.

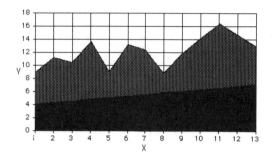 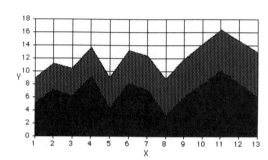

The fairly smooth curve of the bottom segment in the first chart takes on a more rugged appearance when moved to the top of the second chart.

Labels and legends

Labels may be placed within each band, unless doing so causes clutter. The normal method of identification, however, is a legend or key that contains a patch of each pattern and its classification. When using a legend, situate it with the overall balance and proportion of the chart in mind.

The 100-Percent Area Chart

Just as the segments of a column chart can represent percentages of a column that extends from the base line to the top of the chart, so the bands of an area chart can represent percentages of the height of the plot area. The thickness of each band is proportional to its contribution to the sum of the bands, as demonstrated in the following 100-percent area chart, which shows the distribution of arrests among different age groups.

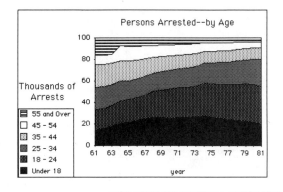

The Shaded-Zone Chart

The shaded-zone variation of the area chart is used to accent a specific band on a chart or to compare two trends within a group. As an example, you might use this chart to stress the increase in crime among young adults.

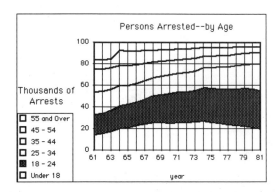

If you were more interested in comparing the criminal activities of one age group with those of another, you could shade the two zones.

Creating Area Charts

You follow the same steps to create a simple area chart that you have followed for our other formats: Choose, from the Data menu, the series type you would like to create (sequence, date, text, number) and fill out the properties sheet. This creates a series window into which you can type the information to be plotted.

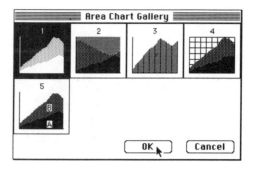

Once you have a series created and information entered, you can choose a specific area-chart format from the Area Chart Gallery and click Plot Series in the series window. The chart is drawn in the format you chose. After the chart is drawn, you can change the pattern beneath the line, add text, arrows, and other enhancements, and send it to the printer.

The Simple Area Chart

An area chart, like a line graph, owes its accuracy to the large number of data points plotted. Because you will have to enter a lot of information to create an area chart, we will work with only one example throughout this chapter. We'll start by plotting one series to investigate the characteristics of the simple area chart, and then we'll add a few more series to study the subdivided and zone charts. Your area chart will end up looking like this one, which plots the age-distribution of people arrested between 1961 and 1981.

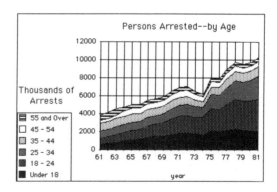

Creating a series

After clearing Chart's desktop, take out a new Date Series properties sheet by choosing Date from the Data menu.

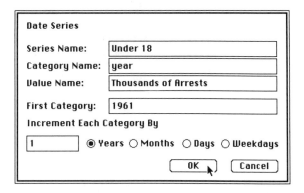

Type in the names and set the first category and increment, as in this example. The series name (Under 18) was chosen to be compatible with the names of the other series that will appear in the legend. Since this is the first series on this chart, the series name will also be the chart title; you will change the title on the chart later. When the properties sheet is filled out correctly, click OK to return to the desktop and a series window containing your new titles.

Entering data

year	Thousands of Arrests
1961	567
1962	653
1963	789
1964	961
1965	1074
1966	1149
1967	1340
1968	1457
1969	1500
1970	1661
1971	1797
1972	1794
1973	1717
1974	1683
1975	2078
1976	1973
1977	2170
1978	2279
1979	2143
1980	2026
1981	2036

Enter these numbers into your series window. Since this is a Date series, Chart fills in the dates, starting with 1961 and adding one year at a time. Each number you type appears in the value column, opposite the next year in the sequence, which appears in the category column.

Since there are 21 entries, by the time you get to the bottom of the list the top has long since scrolled out of sight. To review the list, drag the scroll bar toward the top of the series window. To see more of the list at one time, enlarge the window.

As you become familiar with the Chart program, you learn to anticipate and resolve difficulties before clicking Plot Series. With this many entries, you can anticipate that the category axis will be crowded. You can reduce this congestion in several ways. Choosing Categories from the Format menu and changing the Date Format to Short will help. When you do this, the series window is redrawn with the dates listed from 61 to 81, rather than 1961 to 1981.

Before you click the Plot Series button to display this crime wave, choose Area Chart from the Gallery menu and OK the preset selection. When you click Plot Series, you will discover that your modification to the category-axis tick labels reduced, but didn't alleviate, the crowding below the horizontal axis. To finish solving this problem, select the axis and then choose Axis from the Format menu and enter a 2 in the box after Number of Categories Between Tick Mark Labels. Your chart is redrawn to look like this.

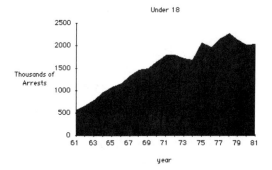

If this were all the information you wanted to present on this subject, you could frame the chart and be done with it, but let's add a few more series to see the overall picture.

The Subdivided Area Chart

The *Statistical Abstract* divides offenders into six age groups: under 18, 18-24, 25-34, 35-44, 45-54, 55 and over. Create a series for each of these groups (other than the under 18 group, which you've already done) and enter these numbers.

year	under 18	18-24	25-34	35-44	45-54	over 54
61	567	703	806	818	329	626
62	653	749	833	869	343	668
63	789	881	875	911	357	696
64	961	959	858	877	644	364
65	1074	1050	891	917	670	421
66	1149	1089	858	857	641	413
67	1340	1274	928	882	667	426
68	1457	1372	931	828	627	401
69	1500	1514	990	823	635	398
70	1661	1785	1128	887	685	425
71	1797	1935	1203	900	697	430
72	1794	1958	1270	884	681	413
73	1717	1869	1179	768	597	360
74	1683	1886	1140	664	500	299
75	2078	2482	1546	870	644	386
76	1973	2517	1589	857	604	367
77	2170	2920	1887	970	665	409
78	2279	3257	2111	1037	669	412
79	2143	3279	2106	983	600	385
80	2026	3426	2298	1001	574	378
81	2036	3594	2582	1089	593	400

To create a subdivided area chart, cycle five more times through the steps used to create your simple area chart. The only difference between each properties sheet is the name, which should reflect the age group to be plotted by that series (18-24, 25-34, and so on).

When creating charts like this one—or doing anything else involving substantial typing on a computer—it is a reasonable precaution to save a copy of what you have entered before you start manipulating it. A power failure is irritating at any time, but it's a known fact that your dog can chew on the computer's power cord every day for three weeks, and won't take the fatal bite until immediately after you've spent an hour typing in a long list of numbers. The first time you want to preserve a copy of your information on disk, you can do so by choosing Save As from the File menu and assigning a name. After doing this once, you can periodically save the updates simply by choosing Save. Saving your chart does not disturb what is displayed on your screen, but may save a little disturbance on your part should disaster strike.

Now that your information is safe, let's have a look at it. Choose List from the Data menu and, for each series you just added, click the box in the Plot column. The area chart format was chosen when you plotted the first series, so when you click OK in the List dialog box, the program creates this chart.

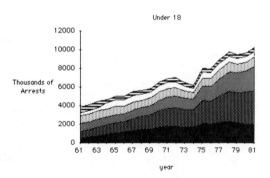

Each of the six bands represents the number of persons in one age group arrested during this period.

The title, which is the name of the first series plotted, no longer accurately represents the information plotted on the chart. A more appropriate title is Persons Arrested—by Age. Change the title by selecting the existing title, dragging through it to highlight the text, and typing the new title. While the title is selected, choose Text from the Format menu and click Medium under Font Size. Then select the value-axis title and enlarge it to Medium as well.

This chart would be more informative if we knew which band represented which age group. Adding a legend is easy; just choose Add Legend from the Chart menu. The chart is redrawn to make room for the new legend, which the program automatically places at the right. The combination of value-axis title on the left and legend on the right leaves little room for the chart in the middle. Rather than moving the title up and allowing the chart to absorb the space beneath it, as we have done previously, tuck the legend into the space below the value title.

To move the legend, select it (by clicking anyplace in it), place the pointer over it (the pointer changes to a four-headed arrow), and drag.

Select the plot area by choosing Select Plot Area from the Chart menu, and enlarge it by dragging the black handle on the right side. Now frame the chart by choosing Select Chart from the Chart menu, and then choosing Patterns from the Format menu and picking an appropriate frame style, weight, and pattern. When the frame is drawn, you may discover that the legend doesn't fit precisely into the lower left corner of the frame. This is remedied by either dragging the frame to make it larger (you just added the frame, so it is still selected; simply drag a handle), or moving the legend.

As a final touch, to break up the white space on the chart, you can add a grid to the plot area. To do this, choose Axes from the Chart menu and click Major Grid Lines under both Categories and Values. Your chart now looks like this.

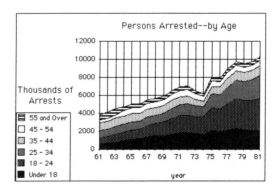

The 100-Percent Area Chart

The area chart you created with this information indicates the actual number of arrests in each age group. To see each group's proportion of arrests you can convert this chart to a 100-percent area chart. There are several ways you can make this conversion. You could choose Area Chart again from the Gallery menu, and this time click the small chart that resembles the 100-percent format (number 2). Instead, use a second method; choose Main Chart from the Format menu and click the box in front of 100%. When you OK your choice, the chart is redrawn to resemble this one.

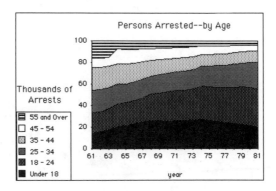

Have you been studying these examples to see what relationships can be discovered from a graph? I chose this information to chart because there was a table of data conveniently available; and then, after I saw the resulting chart, I discovered something that wasn't apparent from the table. Notice how the proportion of persons arrested who are under 18 climbs steadily until 1968—the year the babies of 1950 turned 18. In 1968 the percentage of juveniles arrested starts to drop, but the 18- to 24-year-old group continues to rise. In 1974 the torch is again passed, and the number of arrests for the 25- to 34-year-old group, which had been steadily declining, begins to climb.

Do we have a group of people born in the mid-forties to early fifties who are more criminally inclined than the average? Or not as successful at crime? Or is this simply the sheer mass of the Baby Boom making itself felt? A new chart plotting the number of arrests per thousand people in each age group would reveal the answers to these questions.

The Shaded-Zone Chart

You don't directly create a shaded-zone chart with the Chart program; you create whichever other version of layered area chart you like the shape of, and then apply our invisible pattern to the zones you *don't* want to accent. Let's do that to the 100-percent area chart you just created, emphasizing the band that represents 18- to 24-year-olds.

Place the pointer in the first band and click; the band is surrounded with white dots to indicate that it has been selected for some further action. Now choose Patterns from the Format menu and click Invisible under Area Pattern. When you click OK, the dialog box disappears and the chart is redrawn with no pattern in its bottom band.

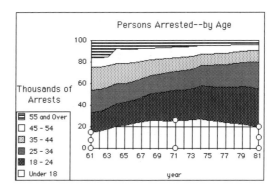

The bottom band still shows the grid you created earlier and then covered with the 100-percent area chart. The fact that you can see this grid demonstrates the difference between choosing a white pattern and one that is invisible. If we had not added the grid to the chart and there were nothing behind the bottom band other than the white background, then the invisible and white patterns would now look the same; but grid lines (or any other background pattern) show through an invisible band and are covered by a white band (as you can see with the second band from the top).

You can repeat this process for the third, fourth, fifth, and sixth bands (skipping the second, which is the one you want to emphasize), or you can speed things up a little by returning to the Patterns dialog box with the invisible pattern still selected, and clicking Apply to All. This clears all patterns; you can then select the second band and give it an appropriate visible pattern. When your chart is redrawn after all your changes, it looks like this.

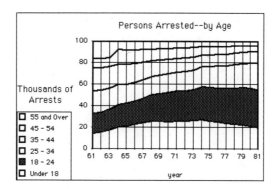

The
Scatter
Graph

To the uninitiated, the scatter graph is the most difficult of Chart's formats. The program will easily and automatically create a scatter graph, and even supply a few tools to help you analyze its meaning, but the relationships expressed by a scatter graph are complex and often buried deep in the data.

The graphic formats I have discussed so far have one factor in common: They all express the relationship of a dependent variable to an independent variable. With column, line, and area charts, the independent variable, called the category, is typically identified on the X-axis and the dependent variable, called the value, is identified on the Y-axis. The bar chart reverses this orientation; and the pie chart redefines it completely, expressing the value in degrees or radians of arc around the perimeter of a circle. The scatter graph does not necessarily express a dependent- to independent-variable relationship.

Also known as the scatter diagram or scattergram, the scatter graph is normally used as an analytical tool to discover the degree and type of relationship existing between two variables. One of these variables may, to some degree, be dependent on the other; for example, the weight of individuals in a group is loosely dependent on their height. More often, the variables are mutually independent; the relationship of test scores on college entrance exams and the grades later earned, for example. The entrance exam scores don't *cause* the college grades; any relationship between the two is due to an external factor— usually the knowledge and ability of the student.

The purpose of a scatter graph is to help you determine whether a relationship exists between the two variables, and if so, just what it is and how dependable it is. If you can consistently associate the condition of one variable with that of the other, you have a strong possibility of predicting the second variable when you know the first.

If relationships were clear cut and easy to interpret, there would be more winners at the race track and in the stock market. As it is, you can rarely be aware of all the factors that could perhaps influence a change; the best you can hope for is a high degree of reliability in your prediction—otherwise known as an educated guess.

Standards

A noticeable visual difference between the scatter graph and most other formats is the relative proportion of the axes. The horizontal and vertical axes of a scatter graph should be of equal length, forming a square, as opposed to the rectangular shape used with other charts.

The axes should be long enough for each to have eight to fifteen divisions, with sufficient room between intervals for the necessary identifying labels and marks.

The standard styles available when you choose Scatter from the Gallery menu allow you to express your data in several ways, as an aid to discovering any possible relationship.

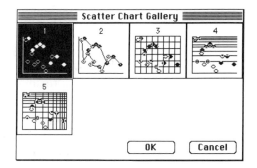

Of these different styles, the ones most significantly out of the ordinary are the last two, which use logarithmic scales either on the vertical axis or on both axes. The scatter graph format frequently makes use of logarithmic and double logarithmic scales to plot widely divergent numbers on the same grid. Examples later in the chapter will give you some idea of when it is appropriate to use logarithmic scales on your charts. First, let's look at the simple scatter graph.

The Simple Scatter Graph

Each plotted dot on the scatter graph represents two values: one measured on the horizontal axis and one on the vertical axis. Unlike other formats, a value on either axis may be associated with more than one value on the other axis. In the graph shown here, the number 10 on the horizontal axis is associated with 3, 9, and 15 on the vertical axis.

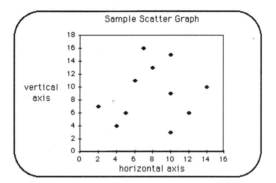

A scatter graph can easily be mistaken for a connect-the-dots drawing, and, without some method of interpreting the information on the graph, it is just about as useful.

The variable measured on the horizontal axis may have absolutely no relationship to the variable measured on the vertical axis, in which case the plotted points appear to be randomly scattered about the grid, as in the sample scatter graph already shown. On the other hand, there may be a very direct relationship between the values on one axis and their associated values on the other axis, in which case the points are grouped together in a density that looks more and more like a straight line as the relationship increases.

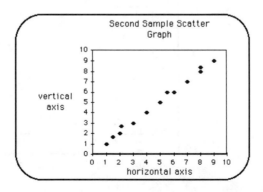

With the other types of charts we have used, it is easy to visually compare the values plotted on one to those plotted on another; you simply compare the length of a bar, the height of a line, or the size of a pie segment. It is more difficult to visually compare scatter graphs, but the relationship of the plotted points on one can be mathematically compared to that on another by computing a *correlation coefficient* (referred to as *r*) for each graph and comparing these coefficients.

The correlation coefficient

The formula for computing the correlation coefficient involves a lot of very simple but very tedious math; fortunately the Chart program computes this factor for you. The value of r is always between −1 and +1. A positive r indicates a positive relationship between the variables; as one variable increases in value, so should the other. If r has a negative value, you can expect one variable to decrease as the other increases. The closer r is to −1 or +1, the more direct is the relationship between the variables. A value of 0 indicates a random association between the variables. This illustration shows four scatter graphs and their correlation coefficients.

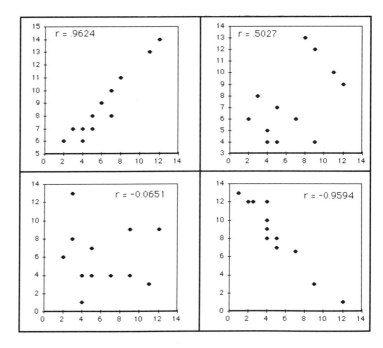

Logarithmic (Log) Scales

The charts we have looked at so far in this chapter have partitioned their axes with arithmetic scales—scales divided into equal-sized segments, with each segment having the same value. The log scale is an alternative that is useful for plotting points that span a wide range of values. The effectiveness of the log scale is due to the manner in which it proportions a linear space. I won't go into the logic behind it, but visually the log scale is divided into tiers (also called cycles, banks, decks, or phases). All the tiers on any one chart are the same height and each is divided into nine increments by ten lines, numbered either 1 to 10 or a power of 1 to 10.

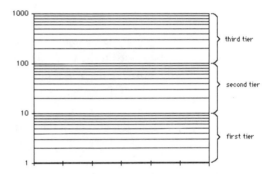

Here is a single log scale with three tiers. Values from 1 to 10 are plotted on the lower tier; values from 10 to 100 are plotted on the second tier; and values from 100 to 1000 are plotted on the top tier. Each increment in a tier is equal to 10 percent of the maximum value of the tier—the second tier is scaled 10, 20, 30, 40, and so on—but the size of the increments gets smaller as they get closer to the top of the tier.

Notice that the log scale does not extend to zero. This is not a problem, as the first tier can be made to represent very small powers of ten, such as .001 to .01, and values approaching zero can, thus, be plotted. Typically, that degree of accuracy is not required close to the base line; the normal starting point for the log scale is 1 or 10.

The log scale becomes effective on a scatter graph when the values span three or more tiers. The log scale can be used on either axis, though if it is only required to plot the values in one dimension, those values are usually plotted along the vertical axis rather than the horizontal.

The Single Logarithmic-Scale Scatter Graph

This graph is an example of a single logarithmic-scale, or log-scale, scatter graph.

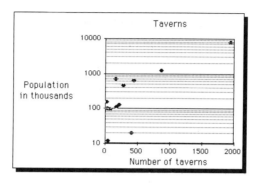

Each plotted point on this graph represents a city. The value on the vertical axis is the city's population and that on the horizontal axis is the number of establishments selling liquor.

Plotting such a large variation in population on an arithmetic scale would clump most of the points together in the bottom left corner of the graph.

Using a log scale requires no special knowledge on your part—you don't even have to understand what a logarithm is. All you have to be able to do is recognize when your information is so scrunched up that it cannot be properly displayed and analyzed with arithmetic scales.

The Double Logarithmic-Scale Scatter Graph

The scatter graph is the only format that makes use of the log scale on both axes, in which case the scale is referred to as a double logarithmic, or log-log, scale. The log-log scale is used when the magnitude of the numbers to be plotted varies drastically in both dimensions; that is, it varies along both the X-axis and the Y-axis.

Following is an example of the log-log scale format. In this example, each dot represents a state. The scale on the horizontal axis indicates the population of the state; the scale on the vertical axis indicates the number of people in the state whose income is below the poverty level.

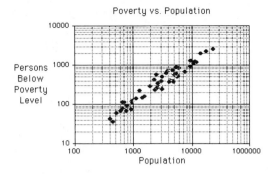

The manner in which the dots cluster to form a straight line rising from left to right indicates a direct relationship between the number of people in a state and the number of poor people in the state—which is no surprise.

You can also see that there are exceptions to a perfect relationship—not all dots are exactly on the imaginary straight line. The dots above the line indicate more poverty per capita, those below indicate less. If this graph were mathematically compared with others contrasting expenditures for welfare programs, job training, and other programs designed to alleviate poverty, you could judge the effectiveness of these programs.

Creating Scatter Graphs

As I have already pointed out, no special expertise is required to create a graph in the scatter format. The only restriction setting this format apart from others is that you *must* define the series as a number series; a number series is the only type that logically plots numbers you have entered randomly in both columns of the series window.

The Simple Scatter Graph

I have picked the data points for this first scatter graph from an especially long table that appeared in a local newspaper. The automotive section of the paper rated about 700 different car models by gas mileage (in miles per gallon) and engine size (in cubic inches).

This graph plots the mileage on the vertical axis and engine size on the horizontal axis. Since neither value varies by a factor of more than about 5 to 1, we can plot them on a standard arithmetic scale.

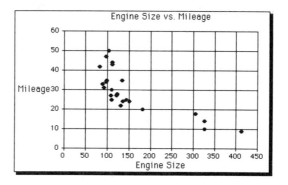

The steps for creating this graph are the same as for the other graphs we have created: First create the series and then enter the data points and plot them.

Creating a series

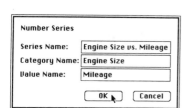

Your first step in creating the series for a scatter graph is to choose Number from the Data menu and fill in the three names on the properties sheet that is displayed. This is the only properties sheet you will need for this example; although scatter graphs often have many data points, they rarely have more than a single series. After you have filled in your properties sheet like this one, click OK so you can continue on to the next step: entering the data points.

Entering data

The table that supplied the information for this chart listed over 700 models distributed among 35 manufacturers. I didn't think you would want to type the entire list, even in the interest of education, so I limited my selections to one or two models from each manufacturer in the subcompact range. I ended up with this trimmed-down table.

Automobile	Engine Size	Mileage
Aston Martin Lagonda	326	10
Audi Cpe GT	131	22
BMW 3-Series	108	27
Chevy Camaro	151	24
Chevy Camaro	305	18
Chevy Cavalier	121	27
Chrysler Laser	135	24
Datsun Nissan Pulsar	98	35
Datson Nissan Sentra	103	50
Datsun Nissan 300ZX2+2 T	181	20
Dodge Charger	97	34
Dodge Colt	86	41
Dodge Conquest Turbo	156	21
Ford Laser	91	31
Honda Civic	82	42
Isuzu I-Mark	111	44
Jaguar XJ	326	14
Mercedes-Benz 190	134	35
Mitsubishi Cordia	122	28
Plymouth Colt	86	41
Plymouth Conquest Turbo	156	21
Pontiac 1000	111	43
Rolls Royce Corniche	412	9
Subaru	109	30
Toyota Celica	144	25
Toyota Tercel	89	33
VW Rabbit	97	47
VW Scirocco	109	25

Since this is a number series, you are responsible for supplying the numbers for both the category column (Engine Size) and the value column (Mileage). Press Enter after each number to advance the insertion point to the next space.

At some point, before you click Plot Series, choose Scatter from the Gallery menu and select a style. I picked number 3 for this example. When you click Plot Series, the resulting graph resembles this one.

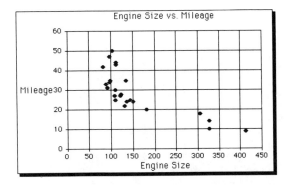

This graph shows, as you probably suspected all along, a direct negative correlation between the size of a car's engine and the miles per gallon you can expect when driving it. You can determine how direct the correlation is by instructing Chart to compute the correlation coefficient. To do this, first make sure the series window is selected, and then choose Analyze from the Data menu and click Statistics.

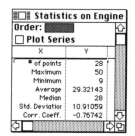

	Statistics on Engine	
Order:		
☐ **Plot Series**		
X	Y	
# of points	28	
Maximum	50	
Minimum	9	
Average	29.32143	
Median	28	
Std. Deviation	10.91059	
Corr. Coeff.	-0.76742	

The program computes a variety of statistics based on the data in the selected window, and presents them to you in a series window of their own. The correlation coefficient of -0.76742 indicates a negative correspondence between engine size and mileage, but not a perfect one; there are a few exceptions on the road, from Rolls Royce to Toyota.

In this example the values in each column are of the same general magnitude, so arithmetic scales work well. If we were looking at a price range of from several thousand dollars to several million dollars, as with real estate, an arithmetic scale on the vertical axis would not be adequate.

Converting a scale from arithmetic to logarithmic only takes a few seconds and requires no special skill or knowledge. The easiest method of conversion is simply to choose a new format from the Scatter Graph Gallery—numbers 4 and 5 offer the single and double logarithmic scales. An alternate method is to select one of the axes by clicking it, and then choose Axis from the Format menu and click the box in front of Logarithmic Scale. Either way, the ease of conversion allows you to try the other scale to see if it displays your information in a more comprehendible manner.

11

The
Integrated
Work Environment

Take a break, for a while, from the restraints of reality and walk with me through the magical land of make-believe.

Imagine waking in the morning to a gentle greeting from your Macintosh; your incoherent mumblings elicit a polite request that you speak more clearly. When you succinctly state that you are awake, the computer displays your appointment schedule for the day.

You no longer peruse the morning paper over breakfast, in search of a significant tidbit buried in the trivia; instead, screenfuls of pertinent information are presented on your Macintosh—information gleaned during the wee hours of the night by scanning dozens of newspapers and magazines, stored in the memory banks of other computers, in search of subjects currently of interest to you.

You don't feel like driving to the office today, so you have the Macintosh phone in and check your electronic mail for messages. There is the usual notice to all employees about cars with lights on in the parking lot, a reminder about the company picnic this Sunday, and a note from your assistant that a minor panic is in progress. It seems that a report analyzing the sales of the company's regional divisions is needed for a meeting of the board of directors this afternoon. The meeting has been scheduled for three weeks, but nobody thought to ask for the report until this morning. You type a short response, saying you will take care of the problem, and then type a few more commands that allow you to browse through the files stored in the company's big computer. After transferring the needed files to your Macintosh at home, you terminate the phone call and settle in for a morning's work.

Your first task is to extract the appropriate numbers from the files you just transferred. Using the Macintosh's word processor, you rapidly scan the files, cutting relevant blocks of text and numbers and pasting them into the Scrapbook. When you have all the materials you need, you quit the word processor and load the spreadsheet program. You quickly copy the information stored in the Scrapbook to selected cells in the spreadsheet, and now your Macintosh really starts to earn its keep.

Using formulas you have typed into several spreadsheet cells, you evaluate the figures for one regional division, computing the division's gross and net profits. When everything works for the first division, you copy the formulas to empty columns set aside for each of the other divisions and watch as their results are instantly computed. After you have fed the profits for each division through another formula that compensates for regional economic fluctuations, and have indexed the last five years on the value of the dollar in 1977, it becomes obvious that the apparent profits of the southwestern division are really the result of inflation, rather than an aggressive sales effort.

The numbers are enlightening, but you're not sure that by themselves they'll keep the attention of the board long enough to prove the point. The numbers will make good reference material though, so you neatly rearrange the pertinent portion of the spreadsheet and copy it to the Scrapbook, to append to your report later.

The results of your computations would be much easier to understand if presented as charts. You copy another page of information from the spreadsheet into the Scrapbook, this time only taking the text and values you want on the charts. Quitting the spreadsheet program, you bring up Chart, create several data series, paste the appropriate numbers into each series, and try out different chart formats. After settling on two column charts, one showing the apparent profits and the other the profits adjusted for inflation, you store a copy of each chart in the Scrapbook and return to the word-processing program.

You're in the home stretch now. You type the report, pausing to paste the charts from the Scrapbook into the proper places and to tack the spreadsheet section on at the end. After a final review to make sure everything looks right, you telecommunicate the report to the laser printer at the office, with instructions to print ten copies and authorization to add your signature (electronically stored in a file at the office) at the end of each copy. You've saved the day, and it isn't even noon yet.

The Big Question

Our little trip is over. Was it really far-fetched fantasy, or just reality stretched to its present limit?

The Macintosh has broken new ground in the easy, cost-effective use of computing power. It is destined to be the vehicle that breaches the wall of mystique surrounding conventional computers, making it possible for us all to fearlessly use this tremendous power.

As the Macintosh was being created, Apple shared its specifications with major software developers in an effort to ensure that an adequate base of application programs would be available when the machine was released. This effort was successful; the base is adequate. There is also every indication, as developers announce new hardware and software products, that this base will rapidly mushroom.

The opening scenario stretched reality very little. Each activity described is possible right now; most can even be done with currently available programs on a stock Macintosh.

The remainder of this chapter will guide you, in a general manner, along several of the paths information can take as it wends its way through the Macintosh. For more detailed information about stops along the way, consult either the documentation that comes with each program, or a book such as this one that concentrates on a specific program.

Communications

We are living in an information age. The storage, retrieval, and dissemination of information plays a key role in almost every aspect of our lives—from the efficient utilization of agricultural resources to optimize food production to the quality of medical care we receive at the hospital. The marriage of the computer and the telephone has brought forth a number of new industries based on satisfying the need for rapid, accurate communication of information. With the addition of a modem and a communications program, you can use your Macintosh to take advantage of the services these companies offer.

E-Mail

E-Mail, short for electronic mail, is an organized method of passing messages between computers. These computers may be linked permanently to an E-Mail system, in which case the message you send appears almost instantly at the addressee's computer, or they may be linked only at the convenience of either the message sender or receiver. The difference between these two methods is similar to the difference between having your written mail delivered to your home or having it delivered to your post office box.

E-COM

E-COM, an acronym for Electronic Computer Originated Mail, is a form of mail delivery offered since 1982 by the U.S. Postal Service.

Using E-COM, you can create a letter with your word processor and then telecommunicate the letter and a list of people to whom you would like it delivered to a special branch of the Post Office. The P.O. prints the letters, merges them with the list of addresses, stuffs them in envelopes, and guarantees that they will be delivered within 48 hours—all for 26 cents for a single-page letter or 32 cents for a two-page letter.

The information you send to the P.O. must be in the format that its computers can understand. There are programs available that convert letters generated by MacWrite or Word to the proper format, or you can go through an intermediary service that converts them for you for a fee.

E-COM is an excellent method of communicating rapidly with a large group of people.

Information Utilities

The answer to almost any question you can imagine is lurking in a computer someplace, and telecommunication is the tool that allows you to pry it loose. By dialing the right data base, you can have instant access to the contents of thousands of magazines and newspapers, all of which have been indexed cover to cover, allowing you to find all references to any subject. Current and historical financial and statistical information about thousands of companies is also stored in this manner.

A copy of any of this information can easily be brought into your Macintosh and stored on disk for further manipulation and use. Once stored in your computer, you can use Word or MacWrite to rearrange the information in the proper format for loading into a database program, such as File, an electronic-spreadsheet program, such as Multiplan, or a business graphics program, such as Chart. It can then be used in the same manner as information you enter from the keyboard.

Electronic Spreadsheets

Electronic spreadsheet programs are electronic versions of the spreadsheet that is so familiar to bookkeepers and accountants. Unlike its paper counterpart, which allows you to record only the results of your calculations, electronic spreadsheets allow you to create a financial model composed of the formulas required to compute the results. You can easily investigate the effect of changing conditions by plugging different variables into the formulas. Electronic spreadsheets are often referred to as "what if" programs, because they can instantly show the answer to the question, "What if I changed this item?"

Microsoft has developed a version of Multiplan, their spreadsheet program, for the Macintosh. It takes advantage of the machine's speed and ease of use to allow you to describe mathematical relationships and investigate the result of changing various parameters within the relationships. Although this program can't do anything for you that you could not ultimately do for yourself with a sharp pencil, an eraser, a pad of paper, and a book of tables and formulas, it does it much faster and will make far fewer mistakes.

Multiplan could easily become the starting point for most of your charts. In this brief introduction to Multiplan, I will demonstrate a few of its features by creating a small financial model and then transferring part of the information it contains to the Chart program for plotting.

Starting Multiplan

The Multiplan program is started just as any other Macintosh application—by inserting the appropriate disk, opening the disk icon, and opening the Multiplan icon.

The desktop you are presented with is topped by a variation of the familiar menu bar.

```
 File  Edit  Select  Format  Options  Calculate
┌──────────────────────────────────────────────────────────────┐
│ ┌─────────┐ ┌──────────────────────────────────────────────┐ │
│ │  R1C1   │ │ │                                              │ │
│ └─────────┘ └──────────────────────────────────────────────┘ │
│═══════════════════════ Untitled ═════════════════════════════ │
│        1        2        3        4        5        6        ⬆ │
│  1  ████████                                                   │
│  2                                                             │
│  3                                                             │
│  4                                                             │
│  5                                                             │
│  6                                                             │
│  7                                                             │
│  8                                                             │
│  9                                                             │
│ 10                                                             │
│ 11                                                             │
│ 12                                                             │
│ 13                                                             │
│ 14                                                          ⬇ │
└──────────────────────────────────────────────────────────────┘
```

The window filling the remainder of the Multiplan desktop contains an empty grid that is the upper left corner of a large spreadsheet (255 rows by 63 columns). These rows and columns are numbered along the left side and the top of the grid; you can scroll through the entire spreadsheet by using the scrollbars at the right and bottom of the window.

Each row-column junction forms a cell into which you can enter text, numbers, or formulas that calculate numbers using the contents of other cells. You select the cell or group of cells you want to work with by clicking them individually or dragging through them as a group.

The line below the menu bar is called the formula bar; it displays the row-column address and the contents of the currently selected cell.

Information is entered into cells by typing on the keyboard, by cutting and pasting from other documents, or, if it has been stored in the proper format, by simply opening a file. For this example we will type the information.

The purpose of this model is to show how your interest-bearing bank account grows when you make regular deposits, and how inflation can erode the buying power of that account. This example may seem a little involved, but it demonstrates that Multiplan can handle complex calculations as easily as it handles simple ones.

Of the numbers you see here, only the highlighted ones were entered directly—the remainder were calculated based on formulas using the numbers entered.

	1	2	3	4	5	
1	Interest Rate=	12.00%		Monthly Deposit=	$100.00	
2	Inflation Rate=	6.00%		Annual Change=	0.50%	
3						
4	End of	Total	Bank	After		
5	Year	Deposit	Balance	Inflation		
6	1	$1200.00	$1268.25	$1230.72		
7	2	$2400.00	$2697.35	$2518.59		
8	3	$3600.00	$4307.69	$3846.61		
9	4	$4800.00	$6122.26	$5195.96		
10	5	$6000.00	$8166.97	$6546.61		
11	6	$7200.00	$10470.99	$7877.94		
12	7	$8400.00	$13067.23	$9169.41		
13	8	$9600.00	$15992.73	$10401.28		

Terms

Before I lead you through the stages of creating this spreadsheet, I will explain a few terms. As I said earlier, each cell in the spreadsheet has an address. This address can be referred to either absolutely, relatively, or by name. For example, the cell containing the word Bank is at the junction of the fourth row and the third column; the *absolute* address of this cell is R4C3 (row 4 column 3). If the cell containing the word Inflation (R5C4) is the active cell, then the address of Bank *relative* to Inflation is R[−1]C[−1]; Bank is one row up (R[−1]) and one column to the left (C[−1]) of Inflation. You can also assign a *name* to a cell or group of cells; the program replaces every reference to the name with the contents of the cells it represents.

Entering Text

To enter text or a number into a cell, simply select the cell by clicking it, and type the entry. To enter a formula, first select the cell, then type the equal sign (=) and enter the formula. Formulas can be typed directly, or, if they reference the contents of another cell, you can click the other cell and the reference to it will appear in the formula—you'll see an example of this in a moment.

Click   R1C1
Type   Interest Rate =
Press   Enter

We'll start by entering all the text. If cell R1C1 is not in the upper left corner of the window, use the scroll bars to position it there. Click R1C1 to make it active and type the first text entry, Interest Rate =.

```
 ¤  File  Edit  Select  Format  Options  Calculate
  ┌──────┬─────┬──────────────────────────┐
  │ R1C1 │ ⊗   │ Interest Rate=           │
  └──────┴─────┴──────────────────────────┘
  ╔══════════════════ Untitled ═══════════════════╗
  ║       1        2        3        4        5    ║
  ║ 1  Interest Rat                                ║
  ║ 2                                              ║
  ║ 3                                              ║
  ║ 4                                              ║
```

You will notice that the column is not wide enough to display all the text; some of it spills over into the next column. If you move the pointer to the solid vertical bar separating columns 1 and 2, the pointer changes shape to indicate that you can move a column divider, just as it did on the chart series window. Drag the bar to the right until all the text is displayed in column 1.

Push the Return key to enter the text you typed and select the next cell down in the same column (R2C1).

Type   Inflation Rate =
Click R1C4
Type   Monthly Deposit =
Press Return
Type   Annual Change =

Type Inflation Rate =. Click R1C4, type Monthly Deposit =, press Return, and type Annual Change =. Now drag the column divider between columns 4 and 5 until column 4 is wide enough to display the text you typed.

These four text entries—Interest Rate, Inflation Rate, Monthly Deposit, and Annual Change—are the names of variables you are going to use with formulas; but before you enter the formulas, you need to provide labels for the results of your calculations.

Click R4C1
Type   End of
Press Return
Type   Year
Drag   R4C1:R5C1

Click R4C1, type End of, press Return, and type Year. You will notice that the text you just entered is aligned at the left of the column (left justified); to center it, as mine is, select both R4C1 and R5C1 by dragging through them, then choose Align Center from the Format menu. Enter Total Deposit, Bank Balance, and After Inflation in the same manner.

```
 ¤  File  Edit  Select  Format  Options  Calculate
  ┌──────┬────────────────────────────────────────┐
  │ R6C4 │                                         │
  └──────┴────────────────────────────────────────┘
  ╔══════════════════ Untitled ═══════════════════╗
  ║       1            2         3          4       ║
  ║ 1  Interest Rate=                Monthly Deposit=║
  ║ 2  Inflation Rate=               Annual Change= ║
  ║ 3                                               ║
  ║ 4     End of      Total      Bank       After   ║
  ║ 5     Year       Deposit    Balance    Inflation║
  ║ 6                                    ▓▓▓▓▓▓▓▓▓▓ ║
```

Your spreadsheet now looks like this. You should save your work every now and then—and now is as good a time as any. Choose Save As from the File menu and name the model.

Entering Values

Next we'll enter values for the four variables at the top. Let's enter all the values first, and then go back and format the cells to display them the way we want.

Click R1C2 and type .12; press Return and type .06; click R1C5 and type 100; press Return and type .005.

We want the Interest Rate, the Inflation Rate, and the Annual Change in the inflation rate to be expressed as percentages. We could format the cells one by one, but it's easier to do them all together. While any one of the cells is selected, hold down the Command key and click the other two cells (or drag through them if they are adjacent); all three cells become highlighted. Release the Command key and choose Percent from the Format menu.

Now click R1C5 and choose Dollar from the Format menu to format Monthly Deposit in dollars and cents.

Click   R1C2
Type   .12
Press   Return
Type   .06
Click   R1C5
Type   100
Press   Return
Type   .005

Entering Formulas

You can display a value in a cell by typing it in, as you have been doing, or by typing a formula that generates a value. To demonstrate how formulas work, try entering this simple formula, which adds 1 to the value in the cell above the formula and displays the result.

Click R6C1, type 1, and press Return. This establishes the first value in what will be a string of eight values; the other seven will be generated by a simple formula.

All formulas start with an equal sign. With R7C1 selected, type = and then click cell R6C1; the relative address R[−1]C is appended to the equal sign. Type +1 and press Enter. (Pressing Enter puts your entry into effect without selecting a different cell.) The formula in the cell is replaced by the value 2, which is the value above plus 1.

That was pretty slick, but entering a bunch of values this way is not an improvement over typing them, so let's use a shortcut for the rest. Select rows 7 through 13 in column 1 by dragging through them. Now choose Fill Down from the Edit menu. Your formula is copied from the top selected cell (R7C1) to the rest; each selected cell adds 1 to the value above it, and the values 2 through 8 are displayed.

Click   R6C1
Type   1
Press   Return
Type   =
Click   R6C1
Type   +1
Press   Enter
Drag   R7C1:R13C1

You can see the formula you copied by choosing Show Formulas from the Option menu. Choose Show Values to return to the normal display.

To neaten up the column of values, drag through rows 6 to 13 and choose Align Center from the Format menu. Now that you've seen how formulas work, let's return to our bank-account model.

The formula for Total Deposit

Although the formula is a little longer, the column of values that will appear under Total Deposit is calculated in much the same manner as the values 1 through 8 in column 1.

Click R6C2

Click R6C2. The formula you are going to enter is wider than the column, but what you type in the active cell will be displayed in the formula bar, just below the menu bar. You will be able to see the entire cell contents there and use the standard Macintosh editing techniques to alter them.

To compute the balance in your account at the end of each year, you multiply the monthly deposit by 12, the number of months in a year, and multiply that product by the number of years you have been depositing money. You are going to enter a formula that will produce a value in R6C2, and you will then modify it slightly to produce the correct value in that cell and in the seven cells below it.

Type   =
Click   R1C5
Type   *12*
Click   R6C1
Press   Enter

With R6C2 selected, type = and click the amount of the monthly deposit ($100.00) in R1C5 (the relative reference R[−5]C[+3] appears in the cell and on the formula bar). Now type * (the asterisk is used as a multiplication sign) and type 12. Finish the formula by typing another * and clicking the first year (1) in R6C1. Press Enter and the value 1200 is highlighted in R6C2; this is 12 months of deposits at $100 per month.

Formula bar:
=R[−5]C[+3]*12*RC[−1]

This formula works fine for this particular cell, but since the formula contains a relative reference for the monthly deposit (R[−5]C[+3]), and since the monthly deposit is not in the same position relative to all the cells below Total Deposit, you will have to convert the reference for monthly deposit from a relative reference to an absolute reference.

Changing a relative reference
to an absolute reference

Converting back and forth from relative to absolute references is easy. The formula is still in the formula bar (if it isn't, select R6C2 again); place the pointer anyplace in the relative reference on the formula bar and double-click. The entire relative reference (R[−5]C[+3]) is highlighted. Now choose Absolute Reference from the Edit menu. The relative reference changes to the absolute reference of R1C5.

Press Enter to reset the formula, then drag through the block of cells from R6C2 through R13C2 to select them, and choose Fill Down from the Edit menu. With the cells still selected, choose Dollar from the Format menu to display the values in dollars and cents. Your spreadsheet now resembles this.

Savings vs. Inflation					
	1	2	3	4	5
1	Interest Rate=	12.00%		Monthly Deposit=	$100.00
2	Inflation Rate=	6.00%		Annual Change=	0.50%
3					
4	End of	Total	Bank	After	
5	Year	Deposit	Balance	Inflation	
6	1	$1200.00			
7	2	$2400.00			
8	3	$3600.00			
9	4	$4800.00			
10	5	$6000.00			
11	6	$7200.00			
12	7	$8400.00			
13	8	$9600.00			

The formula for Bank Balance

The formula for Bank Balance in column 3 is based on the following formula for the future value of regular deposits:

$$T = R * \frac{(1 + i/N)^{N*Y} - 1}{i/N}$$

where:
T = total after Y years (future value)
R = amount of regular deposit
N = number of deposits per year
Y = number of years
i = nominal interest rate

We are going to enter this formula into the cell at R6C3 by clicking the cells that contain the formula variables, typing only the arithmetic symbols used to connect or group the variables. Here is the formula as it will appear on the formula bar (the only symbol you may not recognize is the exponentiation symbol ^, the uppercase 6).

```
= R1C5*((1+ R1C2/12)^(12*RC[−2])−1)
  /(R1C2/12)
```

Notice that the formula contains both absolute (R1C5) and relative (RC[−2]) references. All references will be entered relative to cell R6C3 by clicking the referenced cells. The references that should be absolute will be changed after the entire formula is entered.

To enter this formula follow these steps:

Click R6C3
Type =
Click R1C5
Type *((1+
Click R1C2
Type /12)^(12*
Click R6C1
Type)−1)/(
Click R1C2
Type /12)
Press Enter

■ Click R6C3 to select the cell.

■ Type = to specify that a formula follows.

■ Click the amount of the monthly deposit in R1C5 (R[−5]C[+2] appears on the formula bar).

■ Type *((to indicate multiplication and start the expression that follows.

■ Type 1+ and click the amount of annual interest in R1C2 (R[−5]C[−1] appears on the formula bar), and then type /12 to convert to monthly interest.

■ Type) to indicate the end of this group.

■ Type ^(in preparation for entering the power the previous group will be raised to.

■ Type 12* and click the number of years in R6C1 (RC[−2] appears on the formula bar).

■ Type) to close the exponential value, and type −1) to complete the numerator.

■ Type / to indicate that what follows is in the denominator, and (to begin the value.

■ Click R1C2 to enter the interest rate (R[−5]C[−1] appears on the formula bar), and type /12) to convert to monthly interest and end the denominator.

■ Press Enter to tell Multiplan you've finished the formula and to enter it into the cell.

When you terminate the formula by pressing Enter, the value computed by the formula, in this case 1268.2503, is immediately displayed in the formula cell. Since this cell, the seven cells below it in column 3, and the eight adjacent cells in column 4 will ultimately display dollar amounts, we might as well format them for dollars and cents now. To do this, drag from R6C3 to R13C4 and then choose Dollar from the Format menu. The amount in R6C3 is redisplayed as $1268.25.

Before duplicating the formula in rows 7 through 13 of column 3, you will have to convert several of the relative references to absolute references, just as you already did in the Total Deposit column.

Select the first relative reference, R[−5]C[+2], by either dragging through it or double-clicking it on the formula bar, and choose Absolute Reference from the Edit menu; the reference is immediately converted to R1C5. Select the second and fourth relative references and repeat the process (leaving the third reference, RC[−2], as it is). Press Enter to put the new formula into effect.

If you now select R6C3 through R13C3 and choose Fill Down from the Edit menu, your model looks like this.

	1	2	3	4	5	
			Savings vs. Inflation			
1	Interest Rate=	12.00%		Monthly Deposit=	$100.00	
2	Inflation Rate=	6.00%		Annual Change=	0.50%	
3						
4	End of	Total	Bank	After		
5	Year	Deposit	Balance	Inflation		
6	1	$1200.00	$1268.25			
7	2	$2400.00	$2697.35			
8	3	$3600.00	$4307.69			
9	4	$4800.00	$6122.26			
10	5	$6000.00	$8166.97			
11	6	$7200.00	$10470.99			
12	7	$8400.00	$13067.23			
13	8	$9600.00	$15992.73			
14						

The formula for After Inflation

The After Inflation formula is the same as the Bank Balance formula, with all references to interest replaced with interest minus the initial inflation rate, plus the increase in inflation since the time you started saving. This formula is a little hairy; you could click the cells and type just the arithmetic symbols, but the explanation of how to do this is very involved; so I suggest you type the entire formula. Do so carefully and you will have an informative spreadsheet. Click R6C4 and type:

$$= R1C5*((1+((R1C2-(R2C2+(R2C5*RC[-3])))/12))^{\wedge}(12*RC[-3])-1)/((R1C2-(R2C2+(R2C5*RC[-3])))/12)$$

and press Enter to tell Multiplan you've finished the formula.

You have already formatted for dollar display, so if you drag through the cells from R6C4 to R13C4 and then choose Fill Down from the Edit menu, your spreadsheet should match the one shown. (If the numbers don't match, check the formula carefully; an alert box identifies the most common mistakes, such as unbalanced parentheses, and you have to correct them before continuing.)

R6C4	=R1C5*((1+((R1C2-(R2C2+(R2C5*RC[-3])))/12))^(12*RC[-3])-1)/((R1C2-(R2C2+(R2C5*RC[-3])))/12)				

Savings vs. Inflation

	1	2	3	4	5
1	Interest Rate=	12.00%		Monthly Deposit=	$100.00
2	Inflation Rate=	6.00%		Annual Change=	0.50%
3					
4	End of	Total	Bank	After	
5	Year	Deposit	Balance	Inflation	
6	1	$1200.00	$1268.25	$1230.72	
7	2	$2400.00	$2697.35	$2518.59	
8	3	$3600.00	$4307.69	$3846.61	
9	4	$4800.00	$6122.26	$5195.96	
10	5	$6000.00	$8166.97	$6546.61	
11	6	$7200.00	$10470.99	$7877.94	
12	7	$8400.00	$13067.23	$9169.41	
13	8	$9600.00	$15992.73	$10401.28	
14					

What If?

You may now change any variable (the interest rate, inflation rate, annual change, monthly deposit, and the number of the first year) in column 1. For example, click the inflation rate in R2C2, type .07, and press Enter. You will see a ripple go through the block of values as they are recalculated; inflation has just eaten a little more of your savings.

For another example, click the year in R6C1, type 20, and press Enter. The End-of-Year list changes from a range of 1 to 8 to a range of 20 to 27, and the Total Deposit, Bank Balance, and After Inflation columns are recalculated. By the 21st year your bank balance, in column 3, has grown so large it exceeds the space available to display it, and is replaced by #

symbols. You can widen the column, and display your total bank balance, by dragging the vertical bar at the top of column 3, that separates it from column 4.

Manually recalculating a spreadsheet such as this would be so tedious that you probably would not do it; but being able to rapidly evaluate the long-range effects of interest and inflation rates could help you make a better investment decision.

Moving Data from Multiplan to Chart

The numbers you have computed with this spreadsheet can be copied to the Clipboard or Scrapbook and then pasted into the Chart program for graphic presentation. If you intend to redraw a chart each time you update the spreadsheet and want Chart to always have the newest information, you can link the chart and the spreadsheet. Each time you load a linked chart, the program automatically opens the file it is linked to and checks for changes in the data.

To demonstrate how to transfer data from Multiplan to Chart, we will create a chart based on this spreadsheet. If you have been experimenting with "what if" scenarios, return the variables to their original values: $100-per-month deposits that earn 12-percent interest with a 6-percent inflation rate that increases .5 percent per year. Make sure the first year is set to 1, and select all four columns by dragging from R6C1 to R13C4. Choose Copy from the Edit menu. The information displayed in the selected cells is copied to the Clipboard. You can confirm this by choosing Show Clipboard from the Edit menu; you will see a notation that an eight-row by four-column block of information is stored there.

You may now save your changes and quit the Multiplan program. When you return to the Macintosh desktop, eject the Multiplan disk and, without turning the machine off, insert the Chart disk and start that program.

Although we are transferring four columns from Multiplan, only three—columns 2, 3, and 4—contain data to be plotted; the numbers in column 1 show the time span of the chart, and therefore should appear as category labels for each of the columns of data points. If you specify a Text or Number series, Chart will arrange the numbers in the first column as category labels for the remaining columns. (If you specify a Sequence or Date series, Chart creates a series window for each column and automatically provides the category labels—either sequential numbers or dates.)

Since our category labels in this instance are numbers, choose Number from the Data menu and click OK on the properties sheet. Now have Chart enter the columns of values stored in the Clipboard into series windows by choosing Paste from the Edit menu (or Paste and Link if you would like the two files linked). That's all there is to it. A series window is created for the second, third, and fourth columns, with the years from the first column as category labels for each.

Series 2:38:4!		Series 2:39:03 AM		Series 2:39:07 AM	
Order: ▓▓▓		**Order:** ▓▓▓		**Order:** ▓▓▓	
☐ Plot Series		☐ Plot Series		☐ Plot Series	
X	Y	X	Y	X	Y
1	1200	1	1268.2503013	1	1230.7169539
2	2400	2	2697.3464853	2	2518.5920534
3	3600	3	4307.6878359	3	3846.6088588
4	4800	4	6122.2607768	4	5195.9600992
5	6000	5	8166.9669856	5	6546.6112849
6	7200	6	10470.993121	6	7877.9387013
7	8400	7	13067.227440	7	9169.4103946
8	9600	8	15992.729256	8	10401.275215

This illustration shows the three series windows arranged side-by-side. Notice that only the numbers were transferred from Multiplan; the Dollar format was lost in the transfer.

Plot these points as a line chart (selection number 2 from the Line Chart Gallery), but don't bother enhancing this chart. You are going to transfer it to MacPaint in a few moments, and take care of that there.

MacPaint

If you have gotten this far in the book, you should be fairly familiar with the Chart program; but what have you been doing with all the charts you created? It's easy enough to send them to the printer—just choose Print from the File menu. But suppose you want to combine three or four charts for comparison, or doodle on a chart to give it a personal flavor? For these and other refinements, you need to transfer your work to the MacPaint program.

Moving Charts to MacPaint

There are several methods of moving information between Chart and MacPaint; at any given moment, the best method depends on what you want to transfer, and how you intend to use it after transferring.

Moving via the Clipboard and the Scrapbook

You can cut or copy information contained in a single window on the Chart desktop to the Clipboard, and then paste it into another application, such as MacPaint, or into the Scrapbook for later transfer to another application. The latter method is the one you used to combine the two pie charts in Chapter 8.

Having edited the information in series windows as you created charts, you should be fairly familiar with cutting and pasting text. Copying and pasting charts is basically the same.

To demonstrate this process, we will transfer the chart you just created with the values computed in Multiplan. If you didn't follow along for that particular example, retrieve a previously saved chart or take two minutes to create a new one for the demonstration.

When you are ready to transfer the chart, make sure that the chart window is selected and open the Edit menu; you will see that the Copy command has changed to Copy Chart. Choose Copy Chart and this dialog box appears, asking if you want the chart copied as it appears in the window, or as it would appear if you printed it.

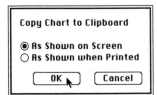

Confirm the pre-set selection by clicking OK. There is the usual whirring from the disk drive, and the chart is redrawn in the window as a copy of it is made on the Clipboard. If you would like to confirm that a copy was actually created, you can choose Show Clipboard from the Edit menu and see it.

If you had chosen to copy the chart as it would appear when printed, the program would have used the parameters stored in the Page Setup dialog box (available from the File menu) when creating the copy. These parameters allow you to control the orientation and size of the chart.

Information stored on the Clipboard remains there only until you cut or copy something else, so your next step is to move your chart to its destination, in this case the Scrapbook. Choose Scrapbook from the Apple menu, then choose Paste from the Edit menu. A copy of the chart on the Clipboard is transferred to the Scrapbook.

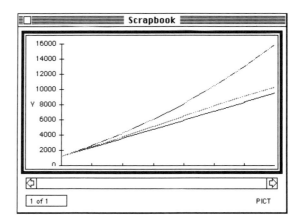

The box in the lower left corner of the Scrapbook window tells you how many chunks of information you have pasted into the Scrapbook and which one is currently displayed. When you have more than one item in the Scrapbook, you can move the scrollbar across the bottom of the frame to view the items one at a time.

The number of items you can store in your Scrapbook is limited by the storage space available on the disk for the Scrapbook file. If you run out of space, you have three options: You can cut items you no longer need; you can move some items to a Paint file and transfer that file to another disk; or you can transfer the entire Scrapbook file to a disk with more space available and start another Scrapbook on this disk (if no Scrapbook file exists on the disk, one is created when you choose Scrapbook from the File menu).

Warning: You can have only one Scrapbook on a disk at a time. If you intend to transfer the Scrapbook file to another disk and don't want to destroy the destination disk's existing Scrapbook file, change the name of one of the Scrapbook files before you make the transfer.

Moving via a disk file of the screen

Most of the illustrations in this book were created by storing a picture (called a screen dump) of the Macintosh screen in a disk file, and then opening the file from MacPaint and editing as necessary to produce the desired effect.

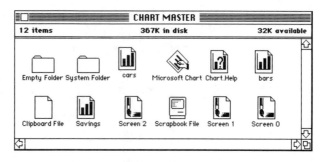

This illustration shows how screen dumps are identified on the main desktop. The paintbrush icon above each file name indicates that the file is compatible with the MacPaint program. The file names—Screen 0, Screen 1, and so on—are assigned sequentially by the Macintosh; you can change the name to something more appropriate by selecting it and typing the new name. You can open one of these files just as you would a file you had created and saved in MacPaint, even though they were, in fact, created by another program.

You create a screen dump by holding down the Shift and Command keys while you press the number 3 at the top of the keyboard. (If you press Shift/Command/4 rather than 3, the picture of the screen is sent to the printer instead of the disk.) The disk drive hums for a few seconds, and then you can continue with what you were doing. This is a convenient method of rapidly creating snapshots of your desktop without interrupting the flow of your work.

Each screen dump requires about 9K of disk storage space, and the machine stores up to ten (Screen 0 through Screen 9) on the disk at a time. If you want more than ten, you can return to the main desktop and rename some Screen files.

Using MacPaint

MacPaint makes designers out of doodlers, and artists of us all. Although this program has the potential for being frivolously delightful and could easily turn into the computer equivalent of Executive Sandbox, it is also a powerful tool for increasing the impact of your business charts.

To completely explain the power of MacPaint in a few pages would be impossible, but I will give a brief description of its basic features and a few examples of how you can use it to enhance your charts.

As with the desktops for all Macintosh programs, MacPaint's desktop is comfortably familiar. The menu beneath the Apple icon is identical (other than the About MacPaint selection) to the one in your Chart program, and those beneath File and Edit contain many of the same commands as in Chart.

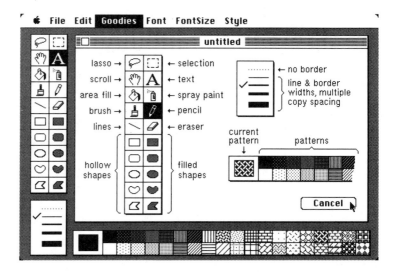

The illustration shown here in the MacPaint window identifies the icons that are permanently displayed to the left of and below the window. The two columns at the left side of the screen contain icons representing tools that the pointer (controlled with the mouse) can emulate, or tasks it can perform. You select them by clicking their icons; the pointer then takes on a shape appropriate to that tool or task.

The lower left corner of the screen displays lines of five different weights. Your selection here, indicated by a check mark, controls the width of certain lines and borders you draw.

The pattern swatches in the palette along the bottom of the screen are available for brushing, spray painting, and filling in shapes. The currently selected pattern is displayed in the larger box at the left end of the palette; you can select a different pattern by clicking its swatch.

The MacPaint window displays only a portion of the 8½- by 11-inch work surface that is available. You can control which portion of this surface the window displays by choosing Show Page from the Goodies menu.

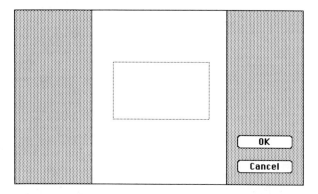

Show Page displays a scaled-down version of the entire MacPaint work area, with a faintly drawn rectangle indicating the portion available to work on. You can move this rectangle to a different part of the work area by dragging it with the mouse and then clicking the OK button. The window is redrawn to display the section you've chosen.

You can also use the pointer, when you have the entire page displayed, to position your project in a specific spot on the page. Just drag any portion of the page other than the rectangle, and all the images on the page move.

If you are going to combine several charts, it is a good idea to sketch the desired layout before bringing the first chart into MacPaint. Working from your sketch, you can then position the window correctly for each chart.

Modifying and Embellishing Charts with MacPaint

You can bring a chart into MacPaint in one of two ways: If the chart is in a screen dump, you open it by choosing Open from the File menu, just as you do in Chart. If the chart is stored in the Scrapbook, you cut or copy it to the Clipboard and then paste it into MacPaint.

Bringing in a screen dump

When you choose Open from the File menu, you are presented with a dialog box. Just as with Chart's Open command, only the documents that can be opened by the program you are using are listed.

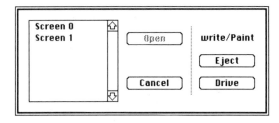

It is quite likely that the screen dump you are looking for is on a different disk—the one containing the application that created it. If your Macintosh has an external drive, insert the disk holding the screen dump and click Disk in the dialog box. If you don't have an external drive, click Eject, and replace the ejected disk with the one holding the screen dump. Either way, the names of the available documents stored on the other disk are displayed.

Click the screen dump you would like to work with and then click the Open button. The screen appears on MacPaint's desktop. (With a single-drive system you will be asked to swap disks a few times.)

If you don't have a screen dump conveniently available but want to follow along with this example, create a picture of the MacPaint desktop by pressing Shift/Command/3 while the desktop is displayed on the screen. The machine hums for a while and, as soon as the humming stops, you can close the currently displayed MacPaint window and open the screen dump you just created (choose Open from the File menu and double-click the name of the screen dump).

If you simply want to modify the chart and then print it, you can now do so. If you have saved a series of screen dumps, however, and want to gather parts of each onto one page, you will have to extract each part from its surrounding screen, store it in the Scrapbook, and then paste all the parts from the Scrapbook back into MacPaint.

Selecting parts of charts

Selecting part of a chart for copying or cutting is somewhat like creating an insertion box for text or arrows. First, click the selection rectangle from the top of the tools to the left of the window and place the pointer (which is now a small cross) at one corner of the area of the chart you want to select. Press the mouse button and drag the pointer to the diagonally opposite corner of the area you want to select. A dashed rectangle now extends from the point where you pressed the mouse button to the point where you released it.

You can now use the Edit commands to move the selected area to the Clipboard and then on to the Scrapbook. You can also use various MacPaint commands to change the size, shape, orientation, and patterns.

After you have extracted the portions of the screen you want, close the window by clicking the close box in its upper left corner. You can now bring another screen dump into Mac-Paint and extract more images or, if you are ready to start assembling your composite picture, you can choose New from the File menu to bring up a fresh MacPaint window.

Bringing in images from the Scrapbook

Whether you are bringing whole charts stored in the Scrapbook by the Chart program into MacPaint for the first time, or whether you are bringing back images stored there by the MacPaint program itself, you use the same basic cut (or copy) and paste techniques.

Choose Scrapbook from the Apple menu and find the chart you stored there earlier. Choose Copy from the Edit menu and a copy of the image is placed in the Clipboard. Put the Scrapbook away by clicking its close box.

You are now back at the MacPaint window. Choose Show Page from the Goodies menu to make sure the window is over the part of the page where you want this particular image, and then choose Paste from the Edit menu. When the image appears in the window it is shimmering, which indicates it is selected for further action. Place the pointer over it and drag it to the exact spot you want it.

By repeating this process once for each chart saved in the Scrapbook, you can create a composite chart. You can then unite the images with a frame, add text, change the size and shape, or even erase selected sections, and add decorative or instructive illustrations.

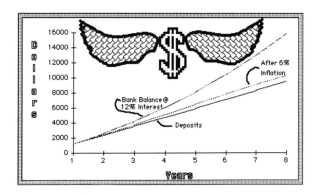

For this example, I used several different font sizes and styles to add descriptive text to the chart, and the paintbrush and paint bucket to add wings to a dollar sign. Turn your artistic abilities loose on this chart—remember, nobody has to see your creation but you.

Once you have your chart just the way you want it, you can print it directly from the Paint program, or you can include it in a letter or report by passing it on to a word-processing program, such as MacWrite or Microsoft Word.

If you decide to pass the chart on to another application, you do so via the Clipboard, in much the same manner as you originally copied it from Chart. Drag the selection rectangle around the portion of the displayed screen you want to transfer, and choose Copy (or Cut) from the Edit menu. A copy of the chart is placed in the Clipboard. If you are not going to immediately paste the image into another application, or if you have several images to transfer, choose Scrapbook from the Apple menu and paste the image there.

MacWrite

MacWrite is at one time both simple and sophisticated. If you are familiar with other word processors, the lack of complex instructions and dozens of commands to choose from may initially make you think it is a weak program; not so. The MacWrite program takes full advantage of the Macintosh's ability to produce many typefaces, styles, and sizes. You can cut, copy, and paste text within a document, and insert text and graphics from other programs.

These features, combined with the ability of the Imagewriter to reproduce the Macintosh's crisp screen image, make this "simple" program much more powerful than many sophisticated (and expensive) programs for other machines.

As with MacPaint, I will not attempt to explain the operation of this program, but will simply demonstrate the ease of including a chart in a MacWrite document.

Starting MacWrite

When you open the MacWrite program, either by double-clicking its icon on the Macintosh desktop or by selecting the icon and choosing Open from the File menu, you are presented with a practically empty window.

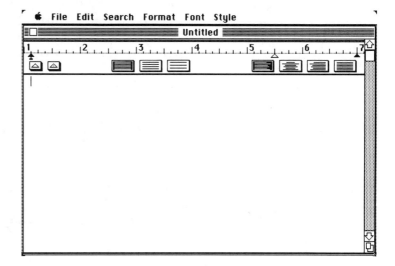

The only thing initially in the window is the blinking vertical bar in the upper left corner, indicating the point at which your typed text will be inserted.

You can start typing immediately. Details such as margins, paragraph indent, line spacing, and justification can be set later by clicking or dragging the icons above the window. As you type, the only special character you need enter is a Return at the end of each paragraph.

Bringing a Chart into MacWrite

The method of bringing a chart into MacWrite is much the same as moving one into MacPaint, except that you are limited to the Scrapbook/Clipboard route.

To transfer the chart that you just stored in the Scrapbook, place the vertical insertion bar in the text at the spot where you want the chart to appear. When you select Paste, everything to the left of the insertion point stays above the chart and everything to the right is moved below.

Now choose Scrapbook from the Apple menu and scroll through the images stored there until you find the one you want. With your chosen chart in the Scrapbook window, choose Copy from the Edit menu.

There is a little humming from the disk drive as the chart is copied to the Clipboard. As soon as the noise stops, click the Scrapbook's close box to put it away. (If you are going to transfer other pictures from the Scrapbook, you can leave it out; just drag it to the side and click in the MacWrite window to bring it to the surface. You make the Scrapbook window active by clicking in the bit of it you see beside the MacWrite window.)

With the MacWrite window selected, make sure your insertion point is where you want it and choose Paste from the Edit menu. Your chart appears as if by magic.

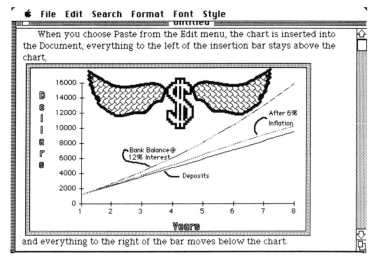

Once the chart is on the page, you can continue to cut, copy, and paste it to other locations in the document. You *can't* type any text on or beside it; no matter how narrow the chart image is, a band spanning the width of the page is reserved for it. If you want a legend or descriptive text to the side of the chart, add it while in MacPaint and transfer it with the chart.

You can adjust the size of the chart and its position within the reserved band by first clicking to select it, and then dragging one of the little handles that appear along the bottom of its selection frame. Dragging the middle handle moves the bottom of the frame up or down; releasing the mouse button causes the chart to be redrawn to the scale of the new frame.

Dragging a corner handle has the same effect as dragging a corner handle on a selection frame in Chart: The diagonally opposite corner remains fixed and the frame is redrawn between it and the corner you are dragging.

You can move the image across the page, in an inchworm fashion, by first squeezing in one side, and then extending the opposite side out.

When you have finished combining your text and graphics, you are ready to print the document. The Macintosh can produce extremely attractive text on printers such as the Imagewriter, with most of the attributes of typeset text. For maximum quality, try printing the document in type a point-size larger than the size you want for the finished document, and then use a high-quality photocopier to reduce the printed pages to about 70 percent of their original size. A 12-point font, for example, reduces to about 9-point, and is very crisp.

For Special Occasions

The charts and graphs you produce with the Microsoft Chart program on your Macintosh are an excellent tool to help you distill an ocean of data for the few drops of useful information it may contain. However, there are times when you want to present your plottings with more pizazz than Chart, even with the help of MacPaint, can offer. For sales presentations, annual reports, and occasions when it is particularly important to prove your point and impress your audience, you may want to engage the services of a graphic artist or other professional designer.

You can still use the Macintosh as the first stage in the production of your graphics. The ease with which the Macintosh can produce a variety of chart formats based on the same information allows you to experiment on your own time—arranging and rearranging your charts and text until you come up with the combinations that best illustrate your ideas. A graphic artist can then reproduce and enhance by hand the work you have done with the Macintosh, using your rough draft for scale and placement. Or you may decide you want a chart reproduced by more sophisticated tools and techniques.

Graphic Service Centers

Sophisticated computer systems capable of producing graphic images of fine-art quality have been around for years. Recently, however, the cost of such a system has dropped from astronomical to merely sky-high, bringing the services of these systems, if not the systems themselves, within the range of the average company. For a typical fee of $100 to $200 an hour, an artist manipulates and enhances your graphic and returns it to you in almost any form you specify—from printed paper to video tape. If you attend a class and learn how to use their system, some graphic service centers will allow you to do the work yourself, at a reduced rate.

Although several hundred dollars an hour may seem rather expensive, the cost must be weighed against that of producing the same amount of work by hand. With proper planning (trial and error on the Macintosh), you can produce a dozen power-packed slides in an hour. Or, if the system you are using has animation capabilities, you can produce one or two short television commercials. The same tasks, done by hand, could take from days to months.

Typesetting

The power, ease of use, and graphic capability of the Macintosh make it an excellent input device for more specialized computer systems, including phototypesetters. Several typesetting systems have been programmed to read text and graphics directly from MacPaint and MacWrite files, and it is only a matter of time before the Macintosh itself will serve as a controller for commercial typesetting and graphic systems.

If you want to typeset a document you have created on your Macintosh, and your typographer isn't able to read the document directly, you will probably have to strip it of all its fancy formatting and telecommunicate it to the typesetting establishment as a plain text file. The typographer inserts special codes in the text that tell the typesetting machine when to make format changes, and what the changes are. You can save on the cost of typesetting by learning these codes and inserting them yourself; of course, this also means you have to take responsibility for the accuracy of the job.

The point I have tried to make in this chapter is that the true power of the Macintosh extends far beyond its ability to create meaningful charts. The consistent manner in which the Macintosh handles routine tasks allows you to tailor your work environment to exactly match your needs. Regardless of which application you are using, you can open and close files, and cut and paste text and graphics, without having to remember a different set of commands for each application. You can rapidly retrieve the results of previous jobs to use as building blocks for the current task. It is as a tool for integrating your work environment that the Macintosh excels.

Index

C

Calculator, 54
Cancel button, 15
Can-of-worms effect, 203
Categories command, 76, 118, 170
Category
   axis, 42
   name, 20, 65
Cause and effect, 153, 179
Changing
   disks, 15, 58
   order of series, 23
   series type, 66
Chart desktop, illustrated, 14
Chart icon, 13
Chart menu, 31, 51, 70
Chart window, 16, 24
   bringing to surface, 19
Charts
   copying, 150, 196, 241
   creating (see individual formats)
   framing, 32, 106-07
   modifying, 26
   moving, 196-97, 241
Check mark, 20, 25, 52
Choosing
   a chart format, 25
   a command, 5
   from a menu, 4-5, 52
Clear command, 63
Clearing format and data, 34, 55-56
Clicking, 2
   creating a text insertion point, 29
   double-clicking, 10
   opening document from mini-finder, 56
Clipboard, 34, 53, 61, 150-51
   moving charts, 196-97, 241
Clock/calendar, 53
   series name, 18
   setting, 53, 55
Close box
   Chart, 21, 23
   Macintosh, 6, 9, 11
Close command, 5, 11, 57
Closing windows, 11
Column chart, 19, 24, 43-45, 91-123
   axes, 96
   connected column, 93
   creating, 100-23
   crowding, 93
   deviation, 98-99, 116-17
   floating, 100, 120
   frame, 106
   gallery, 91
   labels, 95

Column chart (continued)
   legend, 96-97, 106
   multiple series, 93-94, 103
   100-percent stacked, 98, 112-15
   overlapping columns, 94
   placement of columns, 92
   properties sheet, 87
   purpose, 91, 101
   range, 99, 117-20
   separation of columns, 94
   shading and patterns, 94
   simple, 92, 100-03
   stacked, 97, 108-12
   standards, 91-100
   step, 112
Commands. See also individual commands, 51-89
   choosing, 2, 5
   printed in black, 5, 52
   printed in gray, 5, 52
Communications, 227-29
Component band chart. See Area chart
Consumer Price Index, 176
Contrast, 48
Control Panel, 55
Copy command, 53, 62
   copy chart, 150, 196, 241
   copy series, 136, 145, 195
Correlation coefficient (r), 218, 224
Creating a chart
   area chart, 205-13
   bar chart, 133-52
   brief explanation, 16
   by hand, 43-45
   checking accuracy, 41
   column chart, 101-23
   entering numbers, 17
   identifying point, 40
   line chart, 161-85
   plotting, 18
   scatter chart, 221-24
   selecting format, 40
Creating a series, 17, 120, 135
Crockett, Davy, 190
Cumulative sum, 68
Curve chart. See Line chart
Cut command, 53, 61, 105, 143

D

Data
   clearing, 34, 55-56
Data menu, 20, 64
Data point, 16
Date
   format in Chart, 76, 165, 207
   in header or footer, 58-59
   setting, 53, 55

Steve Lambert

Steve Lambert, a native of Seattle, has worn many hats, including those of high-rigger, house painter, locksmith and journeyman electrician. An interest in Seattle's early architecture led him to self-publish a biography of one of the city's influential designer/developer/builders.

With electronics experience gained from his service in the Navy, Steve later became an electronic security-systems consultant to private industry. He has since written about computers for *Interface Age* and *High Technology* magazines. An early Macintosh user, Steve is now a frequent contributor to *MacWorld* and *St.Mac* magazines.

The manuscript for this book was submitted to Microsoft Press in electronic
form. Text files were processed and formatted using Microsoft Word. All
charts were created using Microsoft Chart on the Macintosh.

Cover and text design by Ted Mader and Associates.
High-resolution screen displays printed by George Lithograph Company
from MacPaint files.

Text composition in Caslon, with display in Univers, using CCI Book
and Mergenthaler Linotron 202 digital phototypesetter.

Cover art separated by Color Masters, Phoenix, Arizona.
Text stock, 60 lb. Glatfelter Offset, supplied by Carpenter/Offutt;
cover stock, 12 pt. Carolina. Printed and bound by Fairfield Graphics,
Fairfield, Pennsylvania.